GW00656665

FIRSTS, LASTS
& ONLYS®

HORSE RACING

FIRSTS, LASTS
& ONLYS®

HORSE RACING

A TRULY WONDERFUL COLLECTION
OF HORSE RACING TRIVIA

PAUL DONNELLEY

Firsts, Lasts & Onlys®️ is a registered trademark of Paul Donnelley.

First published by Pitch Publishing, 2023

Pitch Publishing
9 Donnington Park,
85 Birdham Road,
Chichester,
West Sussex,
PO20 7AJ
www.pitchpublishing.co.uk
info@pitchpublishing.co.uk

A CIP catalogue record is available for this book from the British Library

ISBN 978 1 80150 491 1

Typesetting and origination by Pitch Publishing
Printed and bound in Great Britain by TJ Books, Padstow

THE FIRSTS

THE LASTS

THE ONLYS

Pour la fille sérieuse

… comme d'habitude

Introduction and acknowledgements

This is the sixth in the series of in-depth sports trivia books – and there are many more to come. This book will hopefully appeal to those who know a lot about horse racing in the hope they may discover a nugget or two of which they were unaware as well as to those coming to the sport. It should all be reasonably self-explanatory but I have included a brief glossary. I hope you enjoy the book and if you have any comments – bouquets or brickbats – please get in touch via the publisher or paul@pauldonnelley.com. For their help, inspiration and kindness, I'd like to thank the following people: the late Jeremy Beadle; Jane Camillin for her continued faith in this series; Andrea Dunn who caught many of my textual infelicities although to be fair, she couldn't have done it without me; my agent Chelsey Fox; Bill Hartston; Gordon Hawtin; James Morton; the late Lord Oaksey; Mitchell Symons.

Glossary

Allowance The weight taken off published weights carried by horses.

Banker Horse regarded as most likely to win.

Bar Term used when describing bookmakers' odds, e.g. 6/1 bar three means that you can obtain at least 6/1 about any horse except for the first three in betting.

Bottle The tic-tac bookmaking term for 2/1.

Broodmare Mare kept at stud for breeding, and not usually raced.

Bumper Flat race under National Hunt racing rules.

Burlington Bertie The tic-tac bookmaking term for 100-30. Often seen now as 10/3.

Carpet The tic-tac bookmaking term for 3/1. Double carpet is 33/1.

Classic Five historic major races for three-year-olds in the Flat season. The Classics are (in running order) 2000 Guineas, 1000 Guineas, The Oaks, Derby and St Leger.

Cockle The tic-tac bookmaking term for 10/1.

Dam A horse's mother.

Damsire A horse's maternal grandfather.

Filly Female horse four years old or younger.

Full cover Bet covering all possibilities.

Furlong 220 yards (one eighth of a mile).

Gelding A male horse that has been castrated.

Hands Term used to measure a horse, four inches.

Jolly Race favourite.

Mare Female horse aged five years old or above.

Monkey £500 bet.

Nap The best bet of the day from a particular tipster.

Pony £25 bet.

Punter Someone who places a bet.

Sire Father of a horse.

Starting price Often abbreviated to SP. The starting prices are the final odds prevailing at the time the race starts.

Yankee Multiple gamble consisting of 11 bets (six doubles, four trebles and one four-fold) on four selections in different events. At least two selections must be successful to get a return.

FIRST

RACEHORSES IN
THE OLYMPICS

GREECE. 648 BC.

Horse racing was introduced in the 33rd Olympic Games. Jockeys rode their mounts bareback and the horses are thought to be smaller and lighter than those used in chariot racing. When the Olympics was moved to Rome in 68 BC, horse racing remained on the programme only to 60 BC.

FIRST

REFERENCE TO
FLAT RACING

Smithfield, London. 1174.

The first reference to Flat racing in England was in the 12th century when a series of four-mile races were recorded at Smithfield, London. Races are known to have occurred at various markets and fairs throughout the country throughout the Middle Ages and into the reign of King James I.

FIRST

RECORDED RACING
IN ENGLAND

THE ROODEE, GROSVENOR ROAD, CHESTER CH1 1SL. 1539.

Racing was reported at The Roodee, the oldest-surviving course in England, in 1539 (some sources date this to 1540).

FIRST

CARLISLE BELL

CARLISLE BELL, SWIFT, CARLISLE, CUMBRIA. 1559.

Lady Dacre presented the first Carlisle Bell in 1559 with the inscription "The sweftes horse this bel to tak for mi lade Daker sake". The bell was an actual bell that was presented to the winners of the race during the reign of Queen Elizabeth I. Reputedly Britain's oldest horse racing prizes, the bells were believed to have vanished in the mists of time. They were found in the late 19th century in a box in the town clerk's office. They are now in the Carlisle Guildhall Museum. The Carlisle Bell is still run today at Carlisle Racecourse over seven furlongs and 173 yards and usually takes place in June.

FIRST

RECORDED RACING IN SCOTLAND

Leith. 1591.

The first recorded racing in Scotland took place in Leith and was mentioned in the memoirs of the Earl of Huntley.

FIRST

REFERENCE TO HANDICAPPING

ENGLAND. 1603.

During the reign of King James I, handicapping was introduced. To even out the chances of each horse to win, a series of weights were added to the saddle.

FIRST

VISIT OF A
MONARCH TO NEWMARKET

KING JAMES I, CAMBRIDGE ROAD, NEWMARKET, SUFFOLK CB8 0TF. 1605.

King James I was the first monarch to visit Newmarket, the home of English racing. He attended a coursing match near Newmarket and was so taken with the place he moved his court from London to East Anglia. When he was on the throne the rules were written for the Kiplingcote Derby – it appears this was the first time the rules of the sport were written down. There is a record of a race held in Newmarket shortly before the King died aged 58 on 27 March 1625 at Theobalds House, Hertfordshire. He was succeeded by his son, King Charles I, in whose reign **the first grandstand at Newmarket was built**.

FIRST

RACECOURSE TO HIRE
A GROUNDSMAN

DONCASTER RACECOURSE, LEGER WAY, DONCASTER, SOUTH YORKSHIRE DN2 6BB. 1614.

According to early records, racing at Doncaster goes back to the 16th century. A map dated 1595 shows a course where the modern-day track is. In 1600, Doncaster Corporation attempted to ban racing because they believed it was attracting the wrong sort of people. By 1614, racing was firmly established and a groundsman was paid one shilling and sixpence for "making the waye at the horse race".

ONLY

MONARCH NICKNAMED AFTER A HORSE

King Charles II. 1660.

Charles came to the throne after the end of the Commonwealth, 11 years after the execution of his father. He was an enthusiastic fan of horse racing and owned a number of horses. One was a stallion named Old Rowley. The King set up Newmarket, Suffolk as a national centre for horse racing and the Rowley Mile Racecourse is named for the stallion. Charles was known to have an eye for the ladies and is thought to have fathered at least 14 illegitimate children but no heir (he was succeeded in 1685 by his brother, King James II). The horse Old Rowley was equally libidinous and "renowned for the number and beauty of its offspring". The nickname "Old Rowley" soon came to be attached to the King and a ballad "Old Rowley the King" soon became popular:

> This making of bastards great,
>
> And duchessing every whore,
>
> The surplus and treasury cheat,
>
> Have made me damnable poor,
>
> Quoth old Rowley the King,
>
> Quoth old Rowley the King,
>
> At council board,
>
> Where every lord
>
> Is led like a dog in a string.

FIRST

FORMAL RACECOURSE
IN AMERICA

HEMPSTEAD PLAIN, NEAR ELMONT, NEW YORK, AMERICA. 1665.

The first formal racecourse in America was created on the orders of Colonel Richard Nicholls (1624–1672), the first English colonial governor (1664–1668) of New York province. It was two miles in length and was on what is now Belmont Park. Nicholls named the track Newmarket. The earliest record of a race at the course is a porringer engraved in 1668 "WUNN ATT HANSEAD PLANES". The winning owner was Captain Sylvester Salisbury, an English Army officer. A description of the course was written in London in 1670 by Daniel Denton. He wrote, "[There] lieth a plain 16 miles long and four broad upon which plain grows fine grass … where you shall find neither stick nor stone to hinder the horse-heels or endanger them in their races, and once a year the best horses on the island are brought hither to try their swiftness, and the swiftest rewarded with a silver cup, two being annually procured for that purpose." The course later became known as Hempstead Plain and was still holding race meetings in 1909.

ONLY

MONARCH TO WIN NEWMARKET TOWN PLATE

King Charles II, Newmarket Town Plate, Newmarket Round Course, Newmarket, Suffolk CB8 0XE. 1671.

Charles created the Newmarket Town Plate in 1665 with the wish that the race should be run forever. In 1671, Charles became the only reigning monarch to win the race. The race, which is over three and three quarter miles, is run on the Newmarket Round Course (the only time this course is used) on the second Sunday in October.

FIRST

RECORDED WOMAN JOCKEY TO WIN A RACE

MRS MORTE, CHESTER. MARCH 1691.

The diarist of the *Chester Recorder* on 7 March 1691 wrote, "We rode to Farne race where I run against Sir Edmund Ashton, Mrs Morte, Mr Mackworth and Captain Warburton. Mrs Morte won."

FIRST

RACE AT ASCOT

Ascot Racecourse, High Street, Ascot, Berkshire SL5 7JX.
Saturday 11 August 1711.

The racecourse was founded by Queen Anne and the first race was Her Majesty's Plate with 100 guineas going to the winner. Five horses took part. The course covers 179 acres and is six miles from Windsor Castle, which means the Royal Family are regular visitors. Indeed, it was while out riding from the castle that The Queen came across the land that would become the racecourse. On 12 July 1711, her plans for a new meet were published in the *London Gazette*. It read, "Her Majesty's Plate of 100 guineas will be run for round the new heath on Ascott Common, near Windsor, on Tuesday August 7th next, by any horse, mare or gelding, being no more than six years old the grass before, as must be certified under the hand of the breeder, carrying 12 St., three heats, to be entered the last day of July, at Mr Hancock's, at Fern Hill, near the Starting Post." No one knows why the race was delayed by four days although there is speculation that it just was not ready. In 1825 King George IV started the tradition of the Royal Procession at 2pm for each of the five days of Royal Ascot. The Royal Standard is raised and the National Anthem is played.

FIRST

USE OF THE WORD "THRO-BRED"

ENGLAND, 1713.

Now a term to describe a horse bred purely for racing, the word "thro-bred" used in connection with horses first appeared in 1713. All Thoroughbreds can trace their origins to just three stallions – the Byerley Turk (*c.*1680–*c.*1703), the Darley Arabian (b. 1700) and the Godolphin Arabian (*c.*1724–1753) – and a number of foundation mares. Thoroughbreds were created in 17th- and 18th-century-England after English mares were mated with Oriental stallions of Arabian, Barb and Turkoman origin. In 1704, bankrupt merchant Thomas Darley bought the Arabian from Bedouin tribesmen near the ruins of Palmyra. He hoped that the horse might improve his fortunes back in Yorkshire. The horse never raced in anger but 95 per cent of all Thoroughbreds in the world are descended from him.

FIRST

BOOKS OF RESULTS

JOHN CHENEY, ARUNDEL, SUSSEX. 1726.

In 1726 (some sources say 1727), John Cheney produced the first book of horse racing results, now a staple.

FIRST

HORSE RACING NEWSPAPER

Racing Calendar, *England. 1727.*

The first newspaper devoted exclusively to horse racing, the *Racing Calendar*, first published in 1727, contained advertisements for forthcoming races and results.

FIRST

RECORDED RACING IN IRELAND

THE CURRAGH, COUNTY GALWAY, IRELAND. 1727.

The first recorded racing in Ireland took place at The Curragh in County Kildare, Ireland. Curragh derives from the Irish word Cuirreach, which means "place of the running horse". Although used before then — some have races taking place there in 1686 — the first recorded race took place in 1727. The first Irish Derby took place in 1866.

FIRST

THOROUGHBRED IN AMERICA

Bulle Rock, America. 1730.

The first Thoroughbred imported in America was Bulle Rock in 1730 when the horse was thought to be about 21. Bulle Rock had an excellent pedigree. He was the son of the Darley Arabian by a daughter of the Byerley Turk. Despite his age, Bulle Rock was still put out to stud. The importer was James Patton, a merchant seaman, and the owner was tobacco merchant Samuel Gist of Hanover County, Virginia Colony. Bulle Rock's racing career began in 1713 but it was not until 1716 that he recorded his first victory. He retired in 1719. **The first Thoroughbred bred in America** was born to Bay Bolton out of Bulle Rocke in 1740.

FIRST

RECORDED MEETING OF THE JOCKEY CLUB

JOCKEY CLUB, STAR & GARTER, 44 PALL MALL, LONDON SW1Y 5JG. 1750.

According to its own records, the Jockey Club was founded in 1750 but some believe it was created in the 1720s. It was originally a club for gentlemen who were all interested in horse racing. In 1752, a coffee room was built at their new headquarters in Newmarket and it was there in mid-October 1762 that racing colours were registered. Up to this decree, jockeys had worn whatever they wanted. From this time on, they had to wear silks designated by the horse's owner "for the better convenience of distinguishing each horse during a race, and to avoid disputes that may arise from non-recognition of colours". In 1770, the Jockey Club issued its first set of rules but these only applied at Newmarket as they did not have authority over the whole country.

FIRST
RECORDED STEEPLECHASE
County Cork, Ireland. 1752.

The first recorded steeplechase was run between the Church of Buttevant, in County Cork, and the spire, or steeple, of St Leger's, four and a half miles away. Mr Callaghan and Edmund Blake were the jockeys but there is no record of who actually won.

FIRST
RACE BY ECLIPSE
EPSOM DOWNS, SURREY. WEDNESDAY 3 MAY 1769.

Eclipse was foaled on 1 April 1764 during the astronomical event that gave him his name at the Cranbourne Lodge stud of his breeder, "Stinking Billy" Prince William Augustus, Duke of Cumberland. On 31 October 1765, "Butcher" Cumberland died at his home on Upper Grosvenor Street in London. He was 44. Eclipse was sold for 75 guineas to William Wildman, a meat dealer from Smithfield. "Abominably bad-tempered", Eclipse panted like a cart horse; yet, even carrying heavy weights, could run four miles in eight minutes.

Eclipse's first race came a month after his fifth birthday and was won by a furlong. It was a £50 Plate for horses that had never won. A second victory also occurred in May 1769 before Eclipse was sold to Dennis O'Kelly for £1,750 guineas, payable in two tranches in June 1769 and April 1770. It was O'Kelly who supposedly coined the phrase "Eclipse first, the rest nowhere". Eclipse won 18 races including 11 King's Plates. In the days before horseboxes (see 1836), the chestnut colt walked 1,400 miles to racecourses.

LAST

RACE BY ECLIPSE

King's Plate, Newmarket, Suffolk CB8 0TF. Thursday 4 October 1770.

Eclipse's last race resulted in him winning his 11th King's Plate in a walkover. Indeed, of his 18 victories, eight were walkovers. He retired to O'Kelly's stud farm at Clay Hill, near Epsom, and Eclipse produced the winners of 862 races including three Derby victors: Young Eclipse, Saltram and Serjeant. He died on 26 February 1789 from an attack of colic. A post-mortem examination discovered that his heart weighed almost a stone.

FIRST

ST LEGER

ONLY

PRIME MINISTER TO ORGANISE A CLASSIC RACE

CANTLEY COMMON, DONCASTER, YORKSHIRE DN2. TUESDAY 24 SEPTEMBER 1776.

The St Leger is the oldest of the five British Classic Races and was originated by Army officer and politician Colonel Anthony St Leger who resided near Doncaster. Originally run over two miles, the race was called merely "A Sweepstake of 25 Guineas". As would be the case with the Derby four years later (see 1780), there was a differentiation in weight carried by male and female horses. Geldings and colts carried eight stone and fillies 2lb less. The first winner ridden by John Singleton Sr belonged to the event organiser, the former Prime Minister, the 2nd Marquess of Rockingham (1730–1782). The victorious horse did not have a name at the time but was later called Allabaculia. She was foaled in 1773, the daughter of Sampson and an unknown dam. In 1778, a dinner was convened at the Red Lion Inn, Market Place, Doncaster to discuss that year's race. The attendees decided that the competition should have a proper name and the Rockingham Stakes was suggested. However, the marquess declined the honour and said the competition should be called the St Leger. The 1778 St Leger was the first time the race was held in its present location, Town Moor (Doncaster Racecourse). In 1813, the length of the course was cut to one mile six furlongs and 193 yards. Rockingham had served as Prime Minister from 13 July 1765 until 30 July 1766 and again from 27 March 1782 until his death, 14 weeks later on 1 July that year, during a flu epidemic.

DID YOU KNOW?

None of the six horses in the inaugural St Leger had a name. They were listed in the 1776 Doncaster racing calendar as follows – "br. b. f. by Sampson", Colonel St Leger's bay filly by Surly, Mr Wentworth's bay colt by Doge, Lord Scarborough's chestnut colt by Remus, Mr Foljambe's bay filly by a Son of Blank and Mr Farrer's grey colt by Bay-Malton. The Rockingham filly won, followed by the Surly filly and the Doge colt.

FIRST

RECORDED CASE OF A HORSE BEING NOBBLED

MISS NIGHTINGALE. 1778.

Expected to win a big race, the filly Miss Nightingale was discovered dead in her horsebox just before the event. A post-mortem examination showed that she had two pounds of duck shot lodged in her intestines.

FIRST

THE OAKS

EPSOM DOWNS, SURREY. FRIDAY 14 MAY 1779.

In 1779, the 12th Earl of Derby (1752–1834) created a race at Epsom for three-year-old fillies which he named The Oaks. It was run over a one-and-a-half-mile course. The race was won by Derby's horse Bridget. At the post-race party, it was decided to introduce a race for three-year-olds of both sexes. Bridget was foaled in 1776, the daughter of Herod and Jemima, and her first race was the inaugural running of The Oaks as the 5/2 favourite. She was ridden by Richard Goodison who was the winning jockey in the first three runnings of The Oaks. Bridget died in 1798.

FIRST

DERBY

EPSOM DOWNS, SURREY. THURSDAY 4 MAY 1780.

A year after The Oaks, the first Derby was instigated by the 28-year-old Earl of Derby and his friend Sir Charles Bunbury (1740–1821), the sixth baronet. The two men decided that the race should be for three-year-olds and in a nod to gentlemanly manners it was decided that colts should carry eight stone but fillies only 7st 11lb. The inaugural race took place over a mile and this was the practice in 1781, 1782 and 1783. The Derby was run for the first time over the familiar one mile four furlongs in 1784. There were nine horses in the first race. The first winner was Sir Charles Bunbury's horse Diomed, who went into the race as the 6/4 favourite. The winning jockey was Sam Arnull (1760–1800). He wore "a black velvet cap with a long French peak, and a bow of black satin riband behind long hair falling to the shoulders, a white cambric handkerchief, in ample folds, tied at the back; a long body coat with flaps, wide skirts opening at the sides as well as before and behind knee-breeches strapped just below the knee white cotton stockings, Oxford shoes and silver buckles". The breeches are now on display at the Jockey Club's headquarters.

To ensure public interest, a cockfight was arranged following the race but despite this entertainment only around 5,000 people turned up to watch. Standing 15 hands 3 inches tall, Diomed was foaled in 1777, the son of Florizel and Mare. He won 11 out of 19 races he took part in, was second four times and third three times. When his racing days were over, Diomed was put out to stud. As he aged, he became less in demand for his studly work. When he was 21, Sir Charles sold Diomed to Colonel John Hoomes of Bowling Green, Virginia, America. He received a whole new lease of life in the States and was one of the most important studs in early American bloodstock. He died at the age of 31 and it was said, "There was as much mourning over his demise as there was at the death of George Washington."

DID YOU KNOW?

The Derby got its name supposedly after a coin toss between the Earl of Derby and Sir Charles Bunbury when the two men could not decide on a name. However, there is no compelling evidence that this momentous event actually happened. Some have suggested that Bunbury merely deferred to his social superior and let Lord Derby put his name to the race.

FIRST

RECORDED RACE AT CATTERICK

Catterick Bridge Racecourse, Catterick Bridge, Richmond, North Yorkshire DL10 7PE. Tuesday 22 April 1783.

Catterick Racecourse is a popular racing venue in the north of England, 13 miles from Darlington. Racing is believed to have occurred there as early as the mid-17th century. The first recorded meeting took place on 22 April 1783, 30 years before a permanent course was built.

FIRST

HANDICAP

Oatlands Stakes, Ascot Racecourse, High Street, Ascot, Berkshire SL5 7JX. 1791.

The first public handicap race was the Oatlands Stakes held at Ascot, 80 years after the founding of the course.

FIRST

OFFICIAL RACECOURSE BOOKMAKER

Mr Ogden, Newmarket Racecourse, Newmarket, Suffolk CB8 0TF. 1795.

In 1795 at Newmarket, a Mr Ogden became the first official bookie at a racecourse.

FIRST

HORSE TO WIN THE DERBY AND ST LEGER

Champion, Derby, Epsom Racecourse, Epsom, Surrey. Thursday 29 May 1800; St Leger, Doncaster Racecourse, Leger Way, Doncaster, Yorkshire DN2 6BB. Tuesday 23 September 1800.

Champion, a wonder horse, was foaled in 1797 at Oxton Hall near Tadcaster, North Yorkshire, the son of Potooooooooo (Pot-8-Os) and Huncamunca. His first race was in May 1800, the Derby, and he won.

In the autumn, he won the 25th St Leger. Ridden by Frank Buckle, 2/1 Champion beat nine other horses. It was the first time a horse had won the Derby and the St Leger and it was a feat that would not be repeated until Surplice in 1848. In a career consisting of nine races, Champion won six of them. His last and ninth race was on 28 May 1802 and he was injured in his final race and retired.

FIRST

AUSTRALIAN RACEHORSE

NEW SOUTH WALES, AUSTRALIA.
SEPTEMBER 1800.

The first racehorse in Australia was Northumberland, a stallion, imported aboard HMS *Buffalo*.

FIRST

FILLY TO WIN
THE DERBY

Epsom Racecourse, Epsom, Surrey.
Thursday 21 May 1801.

Eleanor, by Whiskey out of Young Giantess, was the first filly to win the Derby, beating ten other competitors. Ridden by John Saunders, Eleanor was bred by Sir Charles Bunbury and trained by Jem Frost. The first prize was £1,102 10s (£106,000 at 2023 values).

ONLY

US PRESIDENT TO FIGHT A
DUEL OVER A HORSE RACE

ANDREW JACKSON, ADAIRVILLE, LOGAN COUNTY, KENTUCKY, UNITED STATES OF AMERICA. FRIDAY 30 MAY 1806.

Lawyer, general, seventh president of the United States, from 1829 to 1837, and horse owner, Andrew Jackson (1767–1845) had a $2,000 bet in 1805 with Captain Joseph Erwin. Jackson's horse Truxton was due to race Erwin's horse, Ploughboy. Prior to the race, an agreement was reached that if either owner pulled their horse, they would owe the other $800. When Erwin's horse dropped out after it went lame, Jackson and the captain could not agree on how the money should be paid. A bitter argument ensued and others became involved. Erwin's son Charles Dickinson began to argue with a friend of the future president, which got Jackson involved. Jackson then heard that Dickinson had insulted Mrs Jackson. Dickinson said he did not recall maligning Rachel Jackson but if he had, then he was probably drunk at the time and he apologised. Jackson accepted the apology but bad blood remained between the two men. In a letter, Dickinson called Jackson a "coward and an equivocator".

The situation worsened and in May 1806 Dickinson slammed Jackson as a "worthless scoundrel … a poltroon and a coward" in the *Nashville Review*. Jackson demanded "satisfaction due me for the insults offered". Later that month, the two men repaired to Adairville, Kentucky, near the Tennessee border, since duelling in Tennessee was against the law. Dickinson fired first from 24 paces and hit Jackson in the chest but did not disable him. The rules stated that Dickinson had to stand still as Jackson took aim. Jackson's shot hit Dickinson in the intestines. He died, aged 25, the next day from his wounds. His 19-year-old wife, Jane, was pregnant at the time of his death. The bullet remained in Jackson's chest for the rest of his life after doctors deemed it too dangerous to operate.

FIRST

GOLD CUP

ASCOT RACECOURSE, HIGH STREET, ASCOT, BERKSHIRE SL5 7JX. THURSDAY 11 JUNE 1807.

The inaugural Gold Cup (it is not the Ascot Gold Cup) was run in 1807 and won by three-year-old Master Jackey and watched by King George III, Queen Charlotte and the Prince Regent. The prize was a gold cup worth 100 guineas. Bizarre was **the first horse to win the Gold Cup two years in a row** – in 1824 and 1825. This has been accomplished several times since and Yeats has won it four years in a row: 2006, 2007, 2008 and 2009. The most successful jockey is Lester Piggott with 11 wins – Zarathustra (1957), Gladness (1958), Pandofell (1961), Twilight Alley (1963), Fighting Charlie (1965), Sagaro (1975, 1976, 1977), Le Moss (1979) and Ardross (1981, 1982). The Gold Cup is run over two miles three furlongs and 210 yards each June. The Gold Cup of 1844 was attended by Tsar Nicholas I of Russia and the winner that year had no name so was called The Emperor. He also won in 1845. Both years he was ridden by George Whitehouse. Nicholas gave a trophy worth £500 (£78,000 at 2023 values) for the winner, The Emperor's Plate, and that was awarded from 1845 until 1854 when the Crimean War necessitated a change. The Gold Cup is the first leg of the Stayers' Triple Crown. It is followed by the Goodwood Cup and the Doncaster Cup. **The last horse to win Stayers' Triple Crown in the same year** was Stradivarius in 2019.

FIRST

2000 GUINEAS

Rowley Mile Racecourse, Cambridge Road, Newmarket, Suffolk CB8 0TF. Tuesday 18 April 1809.

The inaugural 2000 Guineas Stakes – the name came from the size of the purse – was held in spring 1809 having been founded by the Jockey Club under the direction of Sir Charles Bunbury. It is a race for three-year-old colts and fillies. The first winner was chestnut colt Wizard (1806–1813), at odds of 4/5, ridden by Bill Clift (1762–1840) and trained by Tom Perren. The horse competed in ten races, winning seven of them before retiring in 1811 and being put out to stud. On 30 June 1813, Wizard died two days after he ran into a post at Elmsal Lodge, near Ferrybridge, West Yorkshire, breaking three ribs and becoming impaled on an iron bar.

FIRST

RACE MEETING IN AUSTRALIA

PARRAMATTA, SYDNEY, AUSTRALIA.
MONDAY 30 APRIL 1810.

The first race meeting in Australia took place when a horse called Parramatta beat the only other competitor, Belfast. Miss Kitty won a trotting race at the same event. As well as racing, the day's events also included wheelbarrow racing, cockfighting, jumping in a sack and a race between three virgins in which the prize was enough calico to make a shirt. The first regular race meeting was a three-day event at the "race course" (now Hyde Park), Sydney beginning on 14 October 1810. The first competition, The Subscribers' Plate, was won by Chase.

FIRST

HORSE TO WIN
2000 GUINEAS AND DERBY

Smolensko, 2000 Guineas, Rowley Mile Racecourse, Cambridge Road, Newmarket, Suffolk CB8 0TF. Tuesday 4 May 1813; Derby, Epsom Racecourse, Epsom, Surrey. 3pm, Thursday 3 June 1813.

Sir Charles Bunbury's black colt Smolensko was the first horse to win the 2000 Guineas and Derby in the same year. Smolensko was foaled in 1810 at Barton Hall near Bury St Edmunds, the son of Sorcerer and Wowski. In a career lasting two years, Smolensko raced eight times, winning seven and finishing third in the other. At the first Spring Meeting at Newmarket in 1813, he won the 2,000 Guineas Stakes, beating The Oaks-winning filly Music and nine other mounts. A month later, he was at Epsom where he was pitched against 11 other horses. As he was paraded before the race there was a spontaneous round of applause from the crowd and *Sporting Magazine* wrote about his "fine eye, the splendid symmetry of his limbs, the grace and power of his action and his perfect docility". On 28 May 1813, Smolensko bruised the sole of a hoof during training and his shoes were changed for solid metal plates for the race. Smolensko took an early lead when the Derby began but was overtaken by Lord Jersey's colt Caterpillar at Tadnor's Point (Tattenham Corner). One hundred yards from the line, Smolensko retook the lead and held on to win by a length. Smolensko retired in 1814 and was put out to stud in 1815. Smolensko died on 10 January 1829, aged 19.

FIRST

1000 GUINEAS

ROWLEY MILE RACECOURSE, CAMBRIDGE ROAD, NEWMARKET, SUFFOLK CB8 0TF. THURSDAY 28 APRIL 1814.

Five years after the inaugural 2000 Guineas Stakes, the 1000 Guineas began at the same course over a distance of a mile. It, too, was founded by the Jockey Club under the direction of Sir Charles Bunbury. It is a race for three-year-old fillies. There were only five runners in the first race and the winner was Charlotte (f. 1811, d. before 1828) ridden by Bill Clift (who had won the first 2000 Guineas in 1809), trained by Tom Perren (also the trainer of the winner of the first 2000 Guineas) and owned by Christopher Wilson (yes, also the owner of the winner of the first 2000 Guineas) who took home the prize, worth £107,000 at 2023 rates.

ONLY
HORSE TO WIN RACES BEFORE BATTLE OF WATERLOO

COPENHAGEN, WATERLOO, MONT-SAINT-JEAN, HOLLAND. SUNDAY 18 JUNE 1815

Copenhagen was foaled in 1808, a grandson of Eclipse, and named after the second battle of that name in September 1807. He competed in a dozen races, winning two and coming third in nine out of 12 starts. His first race was in a 100-guinea sweepstakes at the Craven Meeting in April 1811 and he came third. He won a sweepstakes at Huntingdon at Cambridgeshire on 6 August 1811. Copenhagen's sire, Meteor, came second in the 1786 Derby. Copenhagen retired from racing in May 1812 and was bought by the Duke of Wellington in 1813 and he opined, "There may have been many faster horses, no doubt many handsomer, but for bottom and endurance I never saw his fellow." Wellington rode Copenhagen at a number of battles and at Waterloo where he was ridden for 17 hours continuously. After his retirement, his name was expunged from the stud book when it was discovered his dam, Lady Catherine, was a half-breed. When the Duke was told that Copenhagen was not a Thoroughbred, he said, "Perhaps not down in black and white – but so much more thoroughly bred than most of the men I know." Copenhagen died at Stratfield Saye, the Duke's country estate in Hampshire, on 12 February 1836, aged 28, supposedly after eating too many sweeties. He was buried with full military honours the next day. One of his hooves was removed before burial, to Wellington's fury.

DID YOU KNOW?

Sometime after Copenhagen's burial, Wellington had the body dug up to retrieve the other three hooves but they had decomposed. The missing hoof was sold to a farmer for three shillings, who later sent it on to Wellington. His son, the 2nd Duke, had the hoof made into an ink stand.

FIRST

GREY HORSE TO WIN THE DERBY

GUSTAVUS, EPSOM RACECOURSE, EPSOM, SURREY. THURSDAY 7 JUNE 1821.

Foaled in 1818, at the Hampton Court Stud, Gustavus was the son of the 1807 Derby winner Election and Lady Grey. He took part in his first race – his only competition as a two-year-old – on 10 July 1820 in the July Stakes at Newmarket and won by half a length, taking home 1,950 guineas. In 1821, he was entered for the Derby with a dozen other horses. Ridden by Sam Day, Gustavus was the bookies' favourite with odds of 2/1. Reginald, a colt belonging to the 4th Duke of Grafton, made the running but Gustavus pulled ahead in the final stretch and won by half a length. Gustavus retired at the age of four and was put out to stud but, despite his heritage, was unable to father any champions. He died in 1840.

FIRST

RACING RESULT CARRIED BY CARRIER PIGEON AND DOGS

Memnon, St Leger, Doncaster Racecourse, Leger Way, Doncaster, Yorkshire DN2 6BB. Tuesday 20 September 1825.

In the days before radio and wireless, it was difficult for racing aficionados to quickly discover the result of meetings. That changed for the 50th St Leger, which was won by Memnon, a bay colt by Whisker out of Manuella, owned by Richard Watt. Thirty horses ran – the biggest field to date in the final Classic of the season. A false start unsettled some of the horses but the appropriately named Dauntless took the lead. Then he slowed and various other horses vied for the lead. With two furlongs to go, Fleur-de-Lis fell and brought down Zirza. Jockey William Scott on Memnon guided the horse to the front and won by three lengths in three minutes 23 seconds. Memnon raced 15 times and won nine of the races, coming second in four. He won 2,200 guineas (£276,000 at 2023 values). More importantly for our purposes, the news of the victory was sent to Manchester by a team of dogs, and Londoners received the news by carrier pigeon.

FIRST

DERBY RACE CARD

EPSOM RACECOURSE, EPSOM, SURREY. THURSDAY 31 MAY 1827.

Nowadays nearly every major sporting event has a programme of events – news and information, team colours and the like. The first unofficial race card for the Derby was produced by William Dorling. The race was won by Mameluke by two lengths. Ridden by Jem Robinson, he was trained by James Edwards and owned by the 5th Earl of Jersey, who also owned the runner-up Glenartney.

FIRST

DERBY DEAD HEAT

Epsom Racecourse, Epsom, Surrey. 3pm, Thursday 22 May 1828.

On 22 April 1828, Cadland (1825–1837) won the 2000 Guineas at Newmarket. This made him second favourite for the Derby with odds of 4/1 behind the first-ranked The Colonel at 15/4. The race began with two false starts for the 15 runners. When the Derby finally got underway, Cadland took the lead. Scipio was knocked over by another horse and his jockey suffered a broken rib. Cadland and The Colonel fought for the lead with Zingaree not far behind. The three horses battled it out until the last 50 yards when Zingaree faded and Cadland and The Colonel went across the winning post together. Since the two owners could not agree to split the prize money, a run-off was ordered. In the run-off, the evens Cadland beat 4/5 The Colonel ridden by Jem Robinson and Bill Scott respectively by half a length to take the £2,600 (£362,000 at 2023 values) first prize. The winner was bred by the 5th Duke of Rutland and trained by Dixon Boyce. Cadland died in France in January 1837.

FIRST

GRAND LIVERPOOL STEEPLECHASE

Aintree Racecourse, near Melling Road, Aintree, Liverpool L9
5AS. Monday 29 February 1836.

The precursor to the Grand National (see 1839) was the Grand Liverpool Steeplechase. William Lynn ran the Waterloo Hotel in Ranelagh Street, Liverpool which was celebrated for its fried fish. He made plans for a grandstand at Aintree and the foundation stone was laid on 7 February 1829. **The first race meeting at Aintree** took place on 7 July 1829 and the inaugural competition was the one-and-a-quarter-mile Croxteth Stakes won by a horse called Mufti. With a close associate, John Formby, putting on a hurdling race in October 1835, Lynn was impressed when cross-country star Captain Martin Becher (1797–1863) turned up to take part. He told Lynn that his friend Tom Coleman had been organising the Great St Albans Steeplechase and so Lynn decided to create his own northern version. The first Grand Liverpool Steeplechase in 1836 was won by The Duke, owned by publican Mr Sirdefield and ridden by Captain Martin Becher. There were ten runners in the first race and four made it to the finishing post. The winning time was 20 minutes ten seconds. The Grand Liverpool Steeplechases of 1836, 1837 (also won by The Duke) and 1838 (won by Sir William) are usually disregarded by historians of horse racing, who recognise the first "Grand National" as dating from 1839. A few days before the first race, Lynn resigned from all involvement in the race "due to indisposition" although exactly what that was has never been satisfactorily explained. The man who created the world's greatest horse race died in 1870, alone and virtually broke.

※ ❖◆❖◆❖ ※

FIRST
HORSE TO TRAVEL TO MAJOR RACE IN A HORSEBOX

ELIS, ST LEGER, DONCASTER RACECOURSE, LEGER WAY, DONCASTER,
YORKSHIRE DN2 6BB. TUESDAY 20 SEPTEMBER 1836.

Elis was foaled in 1833 and began racing in July 1835. His career lasted until 12 April 1837 and, in that time, he won 11 of his 15 races. He travelled to the St Leger in 1836 in a horsebox. The usual mode of travel for racehorses in the 1830s was to walk to the event, albeit at a gentle pace. A week before the race, Elis was at Goodwood, 250 miles from Doncaster. The journey would normally take around three weeks and most assumed that Elis would not run. That was not the plan of the horse's owner MP Lord George Bentinck (1802–1848). The politician's groom John Doe had the idea for a carriage to be built that could be propelled at great speed by a team of horses. Elis and a friend, The Drummer, were put inside and arrived at Doncaster three days later. Bentinck had kept his plan secret so the odds would lengthen and he could make more money betting on his horse. Elis was 7/2 behind the favourite Scroggins at 6/4. The luxury travel obviously helped him. Elis took the lead halfway through the race and his victory was never in doubt. Scroggins came second just ahead of Beeswing. Bentinck and his friends were said to have won £24,000 from betting on Elis. The horse ran just once in 1837 at the Newmarket Craven meet where he won 300 guineas before retiring to become a stud. However, he was not very successful at fathering winners.

FIRST

GRAND NATIONAL

FIRST

HORSE TO DIE AT THE GRAND NATIONAL

AINTREE RACECOURSE, NEAR MELLING ROAD, AINTREE, LIVERPOOL L9 5AS. 3.15PM, TUESDAY 26 FEBRUARY 1839.

The Grand National, founded by hotelier William Lynn, was originally called the Grand Liverpool Steeplechase (see 1836) and did not formally become the Grand National until 1847. Lynn leased the Aintree course from the 2nd Earl of Sefton. The first National was a level-weights affair over four miles for gentlemen riders. There were 29 fences and the course was chiefly ploughed field. The Grand National distance is now four miles and 514 yards and is a race for seven-year-olds and older. In the first outing, there were 17 starters and the race was won by three lengths by

Lottery, ridden by Jem Mason. Lottery took 14 minutes and 53 seconds to complete the course – the slowest recorded time. The win gave Lottery a measure of fame and when races were arranged, many had warnings that read "Open to all horses – except Lottery". The first race also saw the first equine fatality at the National. Dictator – ridden by R. Carlin – fell but got up only to fall again, suffered a burst blood vessel and died almost instantaneously. A reporter wrote that Dictator had broken his back and this statement gave ammunition to those who to this day believe that horse racing is a cruel sport.

DID YOU KNOW?

Captain Martin Becher rode Conrad, an 11-year-old running at odds of 20/1, and the horse fell at a fence then known as the First Brook. Becher dived for cover in the water. The story goes that he told spectators he had not known how disgusting water tasted without whisky. Becher got back on his horse and then fell off again at the Second Brook. The fence was renamed Becher's Brook. The Second Brook is named for Mr Power's Irish horse Valentine who took part in the 1840 Grand National and came third, having apparently jumped the Second Brook hind legs first.

FIRST
CESAREWITCH

Rowley Mile Racecourse, Cambridge Road, Newmarket, Suffolk CB8 0TF. October 1839.

The Cesarewitch was named after Tsarevich Alexander (later Tsar Alexander II, who was blown up by an assassin in 1881), after he gave £300 (£13,275 at 2023 values) to the Jockey Club. The race is open to horses three years old and over; it was first run in 1839 over a distance of two miles and two furlongs and won by Cruiskeen.

ONLY

DERBY WON BY A RINGER

Epsom Racecourse, Epsom, Surrey. 3.02pm, Wednesday 22 May 1844.

The Derby is a race for horses that are three years old. Horses that are less or more than three are ineligible to compete. On 20 May 1844, the Home Secretary, Sir James Graham, announced a crackdown on gambling. He declared anyone caught betting in "any booth or public place, at any table or instrument of gaming ... may be committed to the House of Correction, and there kept to hard labour for three months". Usually, there were booths dotted around Epsom, many containing bookies only too willing to offer varying odds on the races. In 1844, the booths were empty. Some rapscallions introduced two ringers into the race. Running Rein was foaled in 1841, a bay colt. As a foal, he was sold to an unscrupulous gambler called Abraham Levi Goodman. In 1840, Maccabeus was foaled and sold to Goodman in 1841. In 1842, Goodman swapped his two horses and in 1843, having used hair dye on the horse, sent Maccabeus under the guise of Running Rein to Epsom corn merchant Anthony Wood to whom he owed a lot of money for supplied corn.

That year, "Running Rein" was entered in a two-year-old race at Newmarket and suspicions were raised with one writer saying, "To speak plainly, the colt is as well-furnished as many of our bona-fide 3-year-olds." An inquiry collapsed when an employee of the original owner stated that the horse was really three years old. One of the complainants was Lord George Bentinck, the third son of the 4th Duke of Portland, and he spent the winter gathering more evidence that "Running Rein" was a ringer. He decided to pounce if "Running Rein" competed in the 2000 Guineas but Goodman kept his powder dry and waited for the Derby.

Five days before the race, a petition was presented to the Epsom stewards demanding that they examine "Running Rein" properly. The stewards decided to let the race go ahead but to withhold any prize money should he win. The race was run at a slow pace in heavy rain. "Running

Rein" did win, beating Colonel Jonathan Peel's Orlando by three-quarters of a length. As the horse was led into the winners' enclosure, "Running Rein" was booed. Anthony Wood was sent for but could not be found.

The Jockey Club made no decision until a legal action between Wood and Peel was settled before Mr Baron Alderson and a special jury. Colonel Peel sued Running Rein's owner, Anthony Wood, and the case began in the Court of Exchequer at Westminster Hall at 10am on 1 July 1844. Representing Wood was Alexander Cockburn, a future Lord Chief Justice. Peel's counsel (Lord George Bentinck was really the defendant) was the Solicitor General Sir Frederick Thesiger (later 1st Baron Chelmsford, whose son would lead the disastrous encounter with the Zulus at the Battle of Isandlwana in January 1879). The judge demanded, "Produce the horse! Produce the horse!" No horse could be produced and indeed it seems that the real Running Rein vanished at the hands of a mystery man called Ignatius Coyle on 26 June 1844. When the Solicitor General tried to show the court a bottle of Rossi's hair dye similar to that allegedly used by Goodman to dye Maccabeus, he was shot down by Mr Baron Alderson. The next day, Wood withdrew his case, leaving Peel to claim victory. Baron Alderson declared, "If gentlemen would only race with gentlemen there would not be any difficulty in the matter; but if they condescend to race with blackguards, they must condescend to expect to be cheated."

Maccabeus's name was changed to Zanoni and after running a few races was exported to Russia where he was owned by Count Branitsky. He died in 1854. Goodman, having lost his cunning plot to land a Derby gamble, died of dropsy in the early 1860s. Lord George Bentinck died, probably of a heart attack, on 21 September 1848 while walking to a friend's house for dinner. He was 46. Since 1828, he had been MP for King's Lynn although he never spoke in the House until 1846 when he spoke against the repeal of the Corn Laws. He forced the resignation of Prime Minister Sir Robert Peel on 29 June 1846 over the Irish Coercion Bill. Ironically, Colonel Jonathan Peel – Bentinck's acolyte in the legal case – was Sir Robert's younger brother.

DID YOU KNOW?

The goings-on in the 1844 Derby were not the only melodrama. Favourite The Ugly Buck was subjected to foul riding, and second favourite Ratan was poisoned in his stable and pulled by jockey Sam Rogers. Another horse, Leander, was struck and had to be put down, whereupon an examination discovered that he, too, was older than three, probably around the five-year mark.

FIRST
RACECOURSE IN HONG KONG
HAPPY VALLEY RACECOURSE, HAPPY VALLEY, HONG KONG ISLAND, HONG KONG, CHINA. 1845.

Happy Valley opened in 1845 and was the only course on the British colony until Sha Tin on 7 October 1978. The newcomer took over as the principal venue for racing. Happy Valley, dominated by British expats, was built on a swamp and the first race took place in December 1846. A grandstand collapsed on 26 February 1918 and the resulting fire killed almost 600 people. Racing occurs at Happy Valley on Wednesday nights and either Saturday or Sunday. High-rise buildings have been built surrounding the course on three sides and the nearby mountains flattened to accommodate Happy Valley.

FIRST
RAILWAY EXCURSION TO A SPORTING EVENT
THE CURRAGH, NEWBRIDGE, COUNTY KILDARE, R56 RR67 IRELAND. TUESDAY 13 OCTOBER 1846.

The first time a train was booked to take people to a sporting event was on the new Great Southern and Western Railway line from Kingsbridge Station in Dublin to a day of horse races at The Curragh in 1846. The railway companies gave free passage to horses and to journalists covering the events and the expanding railways allowed the sport to flourish. The railways connected Dublin with Carlow by 1846; with Thurles and Limerick Junction by 1848; with Mallow, Cork and Dundalk by 1851; with Galway by 1851; with Killarney by 1853; and with Roscommon, Claremorris and Sligo by the 1860s. As one author commented, "The roll-call of railway stations was like a roll-call of contemporary racecourses."

FIRST

CHAMPION JOCKEY

NAT FLATMAN. 1846.

The jockey championship was instigated in 1846 and was won by Nat Flatman. The records for previous years survive so it is possible to see that he was the Champion Jockey from 1840 to 1852 – 13 years in total. Elnathan "Nat" Flatman was born in 1810 at Holton St Mary, Suffolk and baptised on 9 September of that year. He began his jockey apprenticeship at William Cooper's stable in the county. Cooper was regarded as "one of the most upright trainers and best men that ever lived". Flatman was 15 and weighed under four stone. His first race came in the 1829 Craven Stakes at Newmarket and his first Classic victory six years later aboard Preserve in the 1000 Guineas on 7 May 1835.

By 1840, he was the leading jockey in Britain. In 1848, he rode 104 winners, the first recorded century of victories. Flatman was never first past the post at the Derby but he was awarded victory in the 1844 race on board Orlando (1841–1868) when it was discovered the winner Running Rein was a ringer. Running Rein was actually a four-year-old (and thus ineligible) called Maccabeus (see 1844). In the 1840s and 1850s, Flatman won the 1000 Guineas (Clementina, 22 April 1847; Imperieuse, 30 April 1857), 2000 Guineas (Idas, 29 April 1845; Fazzoletto, 29 April 1856) and the St Leger (Surplice, 13 September 1848). From the 1850s, his career declined and in 1859, his final year in the saddle, he won just 15 races. In October 1859, he rode Golden Rule to victory – his last career win. Later that month, he had an accident – either being kicked or falling from a horse – and a lung was punctured by a broken rib. The lung became infected and consumption set in. He died at Woodditton, near Newmarket on 20 August 1860, aged 50.

<hr />

FIRST

"OFFICIAL" GRAND NATIONAL

FIRST

IRISH-TRAINED HORSE TO WIN GRAND NATIONAL

Aintree Racecourse, Ormskirk Road, Aintree, Liverpool L9 5AS. 3pm, Wednesday 3 March 1847.

An unknown journalist called the race the Grand National from the first running in 1839 but it was not until 1847 that the race officially took the name by which everyone knows it. The 1847 race – the ninth – had the biggest field to date with 26 horses taking part. Around that time, there was a prejudice against black horses – they were thought to be timid and excitable. An exception to that belief was 13-year-old black mare Brunette, ridden by Alan McDonough. Brunette had been a successful racer in Ireland and it was thought would do well in England. Brunette overshadowed another Irish horse, Mathew, the son of Vestris. The bookies made Mathew the favourite at 10/11. Other horses included Jerry (winner in 1840), Pioneer (who triumphed in 1846) and Culverthorpe (second in 1846). Mathew was ridden by Denis "Denny" Wynne and by the time the race began his odds had dropped to 4/1 alongside The Roarer ridden by Jem Mason. Mathew was trained at The Curragh for owner John Courtenay who lived at County Cork – the first Irish-trained horse to triumph in the city that had such strong links to the Emerald Isle. Mathew won from St Leger and Jerry with Pioneer in fourth place. Brunette, of whom so much was expected, finished sixth, the last of the finishers.

FIRST

RECORDED 12-YEAR-OLD TO WIN GRAND NATIONAL

FIRST

GRAND NATIONAL IN WHICH MORE THAN ONE HORSE DIED

CHANDLER, AINTREE RACECOURSE, ORMSKIRK ROAD, AINTREE, LIVERPOOL L9 5AS. 4.05PM, WEDNESDAY 1 MARCH 1848.

The tenth Grand National was run on ground that for the third time in four years was heavy due to rain. The race had 29 runners and riders, one more than the previous year and a record. The favourite was 4/1 The Curate ridden by Tom Olliver and Mathew, the 1847 winner, was attempting to retain his crown. The heights of the hedges at Becher's Brook and Valentine's Brook were lowered and the construction of the Liverpool and Bury railway meant the horses had a narrower curve towards the Canal Turn, making it similar to the modern route. There was a confusing start to the Grand National.

After a false start, the horses were not ready and, when they were released, there was a distance of 100 yards between the first and last. Saucepan refused at the first fence on the second circuit and caused mayhem for the following eight horses. The winning horse, a 12-year-old, never had an official name, and his breeder, Sir Edward Scott, disliked him intently, calling him "a fiddle-headed brute". The horse was the son of Dr Faustus and an unknown dam. In lieu of paying a bill, he passed the horse on to a chandler (a candle maker), hence his name, who sold him to another man who then met Captain William Peel at a meet and sold him "the chandler horse" for 20 guineas.

For the next five years, Captain Peel took the horse hunting before he came second in a steeplechase at Birmingham. Captain Peel sold half a share to his close friend Lieutenant Josey Little (1821–1877) and the two began preparing for the Grand National. It was Little's first ride in Liverpool and he had been mentored by "Black Tom" Olliver. After the awkward start, British Yeoman was leading at the second-last fence but The Curate took the lead. Chandler forged ahead and won by one and a half lengths in a time of 11 minutes and 21 seconds, 42 seconds slower than the course record set the previous year. The 15/1 shot Sir Arthur came in a creditable fifth, having spent 20 minutes in the Mersey having fallen in as he was being unloaded from a steamer. The day was marred by the deaths of three horses – The Sailor ridden by William Holman fell at the fourth fence on the second circuit and broke his back. Counsellor and Blue Pill followed suit and both broke their legs – the most fatalities then at the National. Chandler ran in the 1849 National and came in fifth and failed to finish in the 1850 race.

<hr/>

FIRST

PARLIAMENTARY DEBATE
TO WATCH A HORSE RACE

DERBY, EPSOM RACECOURSE, EPSOM, SURREY. WEDNESDAY 24 MAY 1848.

In 1848, Lord George Bentinck (see 1844) suggested that Parliament should adjourn for Derby Day so that honourable members could watch the race. Bentinck had his own reason for wanting to watch – he had once owned the winner Surplice who passed the winning post in two minutes 48 seconds, winning by a neck. The first prize was £5,800 (£656,300 at 2023 values). The race took place on the New Derby Course for the first time, although the distance remained a mile and a half. The Derby Day adjournment became a regular fixture in the Parliament calendar for the next 40 years.

FIRST
JOCKEY TO RECEIVE
A RETAINER OF £5,000 A YEAR
NAT FLATMAN. 1848.

Two years after he won the jockey championship for the first time, Nat Flatman (see 1846) became the first jockey to be given an annual retainer of £5,000 (£761,500 at 2023 values).

ONLY
ATTEMPT AT BRIBERY DURING
A GRAND NATIONAL

**Aintree Racecourse, near Melling Road, Aintree, Liverpool L9 5AS.
4pm, Wednesday 28 February 1849.**

The 1849 Grand National Steeplechase – the 11th – was competed for by 24 runners and riders and a purse at £825 (£135,000 at 2023 values). The going was heavy and soft in places. Tom Olliver, **the only jockey to have competed in every National to date,** was riding the 4/1 favourite Prince George. The race began with a false start and the starter Lord Sefton had to recall the horses. Finally underway, Horatio Powell was aboard The

Curate who was a pre-race favourite and had finished second the year before. Powell was riding in his sixth – and last – National. He misjudged the second fence and The Curate fell, being so badly injured that he had to be destroyed. Equinox fell at the third fence on the second round and met the same fate as The Curate. The third horse who had to be put down at that race was Kilfane, who fell at the fourth fence on the second circuit.

It was the second consecutive National where three horses had to be destroyed. Tom Cunningham on Finch Mason's Peter Simple won the race in ten minutes 56 seconds by three lengths. It could have been so different, however, as The Knight of Gwynne ridden by Captain G. D'Arcy – one of nine debutants in the race – jumped the last fence in second place. The Knight of Gwynne had started at 8/1 and D'Arcy had placed bets on the horse to win. Desperate to win, he tried to bribe Tom Cunningham, offering him £1,000 (£162,556, 2023) to take a pull and then upping his offer to £4,000 (£650,225, 2023), but Cunningham ignored the bribe. There were no official rules at the time so D'Arcy was not punished but he never raced in Liverpool again. Six horses completed the race.

* * *

FIRST

HORSE TO WIN
THE GRAND NATIONAL TWICE

FIRST

HORSE TO WIN THE GRAND NATIONAL IN
CONSECUTIVE YEARS

Abd El Kader, Aintree Racecourse, near Melling Road, Aintree, Liverpool L9 5AS. 4pm, Wednesday 27 February 1850; Aintree Racecourse, near Melling Road, Aintree, Liverpool L9 5AS. 4.03pm, Wednesday 26 February 1851.

An unpromising horse just 15.2 hands high (the smallest horse to win until The Lamb in 1869), Abd El Kader's dam was discovered pulling a coach from London to Shrewsbury and was bought for 40 guineas. Abd El Kader was the eighth foal and was taken out hunting. His owner, Joseph Osborne, was impressed by how the horse was unfazed by any obstacle and wondered if he might be able to race. His first steeplechase was at Worcester.

When he was entered in the National, no one gave him a chance. The 1850 race had a field of 32 – the most riders until 1909 and not beaten until 1921. There was also the largest attendance so far at Aintree for National day. Carrying just 9st 12lb, Abd El Kader, ridden by Chris Green (1820–1874), romped home in nine minutes 57½ seconds – a course record. Green won two Nationals, the second being on Half Caste in 1859, and trained The Lamb in 1871.

A year later, Abd El Kader was back at Aintree to attempt to retain his title before another record attendance. Thomas Abbot was in the saddle replacing Chris Green who rode Hope, who was pulled up with a broken stirrup leather. Abbot liked a drink and died of heart disease in July 1854. In 1850, Abd El Kader was not rated by the bookies but in 1851 he was given odds of 7/1. There were no fallers until the Water Jump and the finish was among the tightest up until then. Abd El Kader won by half a neck.

The horse competed in the Nationals in 1852 (pulled up before the second time at Becher's Brook) and 1853 (fifth). He was travelling to Liverpool to compete in the 1854 race when he broke free of his restraints and injured himself. Such was the severity of the injuries many thought that he would never race again. However, the horse that had shown such spirit when he was a foal was not finished and was fit enough to compete in the 1858 race although he fell at the second.

JOCKEY TO WIN THE GRAND NATIONAL THREE TIMES

TOM OLLIVER, GAY LAD, AINTREE RACECOURSE, NEAR MELLING ROAD, AINTREE, LIVERPOOL L9 5AS. 3PM, WEDNESDAY 2 MARCH 1842; VANGUARD, AINTREE RACECOURSE, NEAR MELLING ROAD, AINTREE, LIVERPOOL L9 5AS. 3.12PM, WEDNESDAY 1 MARCH 1843; PETER SIMPLE, AINTREE RACECOURSE, NEAR MELLING ROAD, AINTREE, LIVERPOOL L9 5AS. 4.25PM, WEDNESDAY 2 MARCH 1853.

The 1842 Grand National did not come under starter's orders until two hours after it was due to begin. The delay gave the crowd time to have a few more drinks. There were 15 runners and riders and the going was good to soft. The favourite was Lottery at 5/1, the winner of the first National three years earlier. Peter Simple took an early lead but a mistake caused him to drop back to third and it was in this position that he was hampered by parts of the drunken crowd who came onto the course. Lottery was pulled up by his jockey Jem Mason. Seventy Four took over the running and with a mile to go seemed to be the certain winner. Seventy Four stumbled at the last hurdle and Gay Lad, ridden by Tom Olliver, pounced. He had actually ridden Seventy Four in the first National and finished second to Lottery. Gay Lad won by four lengths and Seventy Four was runner-up once more. Gay Lad never ran at Aintree again.

The Grand National became a full handicap in 1843, compiled by E.W. Topham, known as The Wizard because of his skill. He also introduced race cards in 1843 listing the horses and the names and colours of the jockey. It also had a map of the course showing the various jumps. The Water Jump had been widened from 12ft to 13ft. The race was called The Liverpool And National. *The Sporting Magazine* said the race featured "a string of horses never congregated together in the palmiest days of steeplechasing. Lottery, Peter Simple, The Returned and Consul were of themselves sufficient to draw a host of admirers." Lord Sefton sent the horses away 12 minutes late and 3/1 favourite Peter Simple set off at a cracking pace. He could not keep up and Tom Olliver pushed Vanguard home to win by three lengths. The horse was given to the jockey after the race and when Vanguard died, Olliver had him made into a settee. Olliver's third and final victory came ten years after this second when he rode the veteran steed Peter Simple to victory by three lengths. Tom Olliver (he added the extra l) was born in 1812 and began riding when he was six years old. He took part in the first Grand National (see 1839) and went on to ride in 19 Nationals, a record not equalled until 2014.

It must be said, however, that many of his races were not successful – he failed to complete the course ten times. Like many latter-day sportsmen, "Black Tom" (due to his swarthy looks leading many to suspect he was of Spanish or gypsy heritage) was a ladies' man who loved to party and to spend money, often leaving him in financial difficulties. He even found himself in debtors' prison like the father of his contemporary Charles Dickens (1812–1870). He took part in the National for the last time in 1858 before retiring to become mine host at The Star pub in Leamington. However, pulling pints did not give him the same satisfaction as the turf and he became a trainer. The cold winter of 1873 did for him and he died on 7 January 1874.

FIRST

WINNER OF TRIPLE CROWN

West Australian, 2000 Guineas, Rowley Mile Racecourse, Cambridge Road, Newmarket, Suffolk CB8 0TF. Tuesday 26 April 1853; Derby, Epsom Racecourse, Epsom, Surrey. Wednesday 25 May 1853; St Leger, Doncaster Racecourse, Bawtry Road, Doncaster, South Yorkshire DN2 6BB. Wednesday 14 September 1853.

West Australian was foaled in 1850, the son of Melbourne and Mowerina, and began his racing career in October 1852. From then until June 1854, he ran ten times and won nine races. Regarded as one of the best British horses of the 19th century, he was the first horse to win the Triple Crown – the 2000 Guineas, the Derby and the St Leger. The first of these was the 2000 Guineas on 26 April. West Australian was the 4/6 favourite in a field of seven horses. The race began in pouring rain and the second favourite, Orinoco, took an early lead with the rest of the field grouped together. With a quarter of a mile to go, West Australian took the lead and held on to win by half a length from the Duke of Bedford's colt Sittingbourne. A month later, there were 28 horses entered in the Derby and, despite "tender feet", the 6/4 favourite West Australian won by a neck in two minutes 55½ seconds, trained by John Scott at Malton.

Three months later, the 78th St Leger took place over one mile six furlongs and 132 yards of Town Moor. Ten horses took part and West Australian won from The Reiver.

In all three races, West Australian was ridden by Frank Butler, who had a superstition of always leaving the paddock last. As the race got underway, Cheddar and Cineas raced in front before Umbriel took the lead. With one furlong to go, West Australian took the lead and won by a neck. Four months later, West Australian took part in the St Leger as the 6/4 favourite in an attempt to become the first horse to win the 2000 Guineas, the Derby and the St Leger (although it wasn't known as the Triple Crown until some years later). Sittingbourne took the lead early on as West Australian stayed at the back. With a furlong to go, West Australian moved up the field and went clear "without the slightest effort" to win by three lengths in three minutes 20 seconds. In a career consisting of ten races, he won nine of them. West Australian died on 2 May 1870 at Haras du Pin, France.

FIRST

HORSE RACE AT LONGCHAMP

Longchamp Racecourse, 2 Route des Tribunes, 75016 Paris, France. Sunday 27 April 1857.

A large crowd attended the first horse race at Longchamp in spring 1857. The Emperor Napoleon III and his wife Eugénie attended after travelling up the Seine on their royal yacht. They arrived in time for the third race and went into the Royal Enclosure where they watched the action alongside Prince Jérôme Bonaparte, his son Prince Napoleon, Prince of Nassau, Prince Murat and the Duke of Morny. Only royals and aristocrats were allowed in; the common people had to watch from the lawn.

FIRST
FOREIGN HORSE TO WIN A
MAJOR ENGLISH RACE

PRIORESS, CESAREWITCH, ROWLEY MILE RACECOURSE, CAMBRIDGE ROAD, NEWMARKET, SUFFOLK CB8 0TF. OCTOBER 1857.

American-bred Prioress was the first foreign horse to win a major English race when she won the 1857 Cesarewitch. The race ended in a three-way dead heat and Prioress won a run-off.

FIRST
MELBOURNE CUP

FLEMINGTON RACECOURSE, 448 EPSOM ROAD, FLEMINGTON, MELBOURNE, VICTORIA 3031, AUSTRALIA. THURSDAY 7 NOVEMBER 1861.

The idea for the two-mile "World's Greatest Handicap" race came from Frederick Standish (1824–1863), the Chief Commissioner of Police in Victoria and a member of the Victorian Turf Club who doubled as steward for the first competition. There were 2,100 spectators to watch 17 horses in the first race competing for a prize of 710 gold sovereigns

(£710) and a hand-beaten gold watch and the event was watched by a crowd of 4,000 people. The first race was won in three minutes, 52 seconds by Archer, a 16.3-hand bay stallion ridden by John Cutts and trained by Etienne de Mestre. The winning margin over the favourite Mormon was six lengths. The first race was not without its excitement – one horse bolted before the event could commence and three of the 17 starters fell during the race, two fatally. Archer, who despite legend did not walk 500 miles from Nowra in New South Wales to get to the course, won the second Melbourne Cup, taking home 810 gold sovereigns (£810) and another gold watch. Etienne de Mestre trained five Melbourne Cup winners, adding Tim Whiffler in 1867, Chester in 1877 and Calamia the following year to his credits.

DID YOU KNOW?

Despite the competition title, the prize for the Melbourne Cup was not a cup at all until 1916.

FIRST

FRENCH-OWNED HORSE TO WIN THE GRAND NATIONAL

ONLY

GRAND NATIONAL JOCKEY KILLED DURING THE RACE

AINTREE RACECOURSE, ORMSKIRK ROAD, AINTREE, LIVERPOOL L9 5AS. WEDNESDAY 12 MARCH 1862.

From its inception in 1839, only one jockey has been fatally injured at the Grand National. James Wynne was the son of Denny Wynne, who had ridden the 4/1 co-favourite Mathew and won the 1847 race (see 1847). On 12 March 1862, the morning of the race when he was due to ride O'Connell, Wynne awoke to have news delivered of the death of his sister. O'Connell's owner Lord de Freyne offered to release Wynne from the race but he was determined to follow in his father's stirrups and refused the offer. A number of horses were withdrawn before the race including Jealousy, The Dane and Brunette. The field was the smallest for a Grand National since 1841 but the crowd was large.

With the going good, the race began and all seemed to be going well – there were the usual setbacks. Thomastown, one of the early favourites, refused at the second fence and The Tattler at the seventh. For a small number of horses there were rather a large number of collisions. Approaching the 15th (the 5ft 3in Chair), Playmate, ridden by John Nightingall fell after hitting the gorse.

In turn, Willoughby became caught up with Playmate and he knocked over O'Connell bringing that horse down. O'Connell fell on Wynne's chest, crushing his sternum. Wynne was carried to the Sefton Arms Inn – later the Red Rum Bar & Grill and the Aintree Tandoori – at 2 Ormskirk Road, Walton, Liverpool L9 0JB. Such was the severity of the injuries that Wynne died at 8pm that night without ever regaining consciousness.

At the inquest into his death, the coroner revealed that Wynne was suffering from pulmonary tuberculosis or consumption.

The first of the five finishers was The Huntsman, owned by the Frenchman Viscount de Namur, Baron de la Motte and trained in France by Harry Lamplugh who also rode the horse to victory – **the first French-based jockey to win the Grand National**.

It was not The Huntsman's first try-out at the National – he had come in third in 1859 and second the following year. The death of James Wynne led to criticism that the fences were too dangerous and *The Sporting Review* described them as "most contemptible".

FIRST

HORSE RACE IN JAPAN
YOKOHAMA, JAPAN. MAY 1862.

English traders landed in Japan in the mid-19th century, and in May 1862 created a racetrack at Yokohama. Three months later, a race was interrupted by Samurai warriors who attacked the race and murdered some of the English jockeys.

ONLY

SISTERS TO WIN
GRAND NATIONAL

Emblem, Aintree Racecourse, Ormskirk Road, Aintree, Liverpool L9 5AS. 3.46pm, Wednesday 11 March 1863; Emblematic, Aintree Racecourse, Ormskirk Road, Aintree, Liverpool L9 5AS. 3.31pm, Wednesday 9 March 1864.

In 1863, the distance was increased by moving the start about 300 yards, which was virtually where it was when the National began (near to the furthest extremity of the grandstand). This meant the distance to the first fence was about a quarter of a mile. The start would stay here until 2012. There were 16 starters in 1863. The race was held the day after the Prince of Wales (later HM King Edward VII) married Alexandra of Denmark and his mother Queen Victoria had declared it a national holiday. The organisers had extended the holiday, and so many people attended the race it became known as the Picnic National.

The mare Emblem was owned by Lord Coventry, trained by Edwin Weever and ridden by George Stevens. Lord Coventry, 25, bought the horse for 300 guineas but Emblem was not regarded with much optimism. She was slow, was called "a weedy sort" who "couldn't win the price of a saddle". Emblem went into the 25th National as 4/1 second favourite but most of the wagers were a vote of confidence in her owner rather than the horse. The going was good and The Orphan ridden by William Bevill took an early lead but reared and refused to carry on before falling. Inkerman fell, got up and carried on without a jockey. He got in the way of the other horses until he decided to leave Aintree altogether. He was not found until night and was several miles away from the course. The Dane, runner-up in 1862, broke his back. George Stevens had ridden a gentle race, giving Emblem plenty of time to see the jumps. She took the lead at the last fence and won the race by 20 lengths from Arbury and Yaller Gal. Just six horses finished the course. Emblem – **the first four-year-old to run in the National** – was the fifth mare to win the Grand National and gave Stevens the second of his five victories.

A year later, Emblem's sister, Emblematic, took to the Aintree course and followed in her sister's hoof prints by winning the race. Lord Coventry became **the first peer to win in consecutive years**. Emblematic had cost him 250 guineas and immediately proved her mettle. The 1864 National is not regarded by critics as one of the best. There was confusion at the third fence and half of the 18 runners left the race there. Arbury was the runner-up for the second consecutive year. The going was soft, the ground dampened by recent snow and heavy rain. George Stevens won his third National despite being in pain from a crushed finger.

During his career he would win the race five times – Freetrader, 1856; Emblem, 1863; Emblematic, 1864; and The Colonel, 1869 and 1870. Both jockey and owner put money on themselves to win – Stevens backed himself to the tune of £300 and His Lordship put down £500 on behalf of his jockey. Emblem was injured and so did not race, leaving the glory for her sister who won by three lengths. Only five horses finished. Stevens used the winnings to build a home at the top of Cleeve Hill, Cheltenham, which he called Emblem Cottage. He died there on 2 June 1871, a day after he fractured his skull while out riding home to his cottage, when his horse stumbled and threw him.

FIRST

FIRST

FOREIGN-BRED HORSE TO

WIN THE DERBY

FIRST

FOREIGN-BRED HORSE TO WIN
THE TRIPLE CROWN

Gladiateur, 2000 Guineas, Rowley Mile Racecourse, Cambridge Road,
Newmarket, Suffolk CB8 0TF. Tuesday 2 May 1865; Derby, Epsom
Racecourse, Epsom, Surrey. Wednesday 31 May 1865; St Leger, Doncaster
Racecourse, Bawtry Road, Doncaster, South Yorkshire DN2 6BB.
Wednesday 13 September 1865.

Gladiateur was foaled at Dangu, Eure, Upper Normandy, France in
1862, the son of Monarque and Miss Gladiator. The horse was sent to
Newmarket where he was trained by Tom Jennings Sr. He began his
career in 1864 but only triumphed in one of the three races he entered.
The next year was a different matter. He won the 2000 Guineas, then
easily won the Grand Prix de Paris where the fans nicknamed him "The
Avenger of Waterloo". That year he also won the Derby, ridden by Harry
Grimshaw, from a field of 30 by two lengths in two minutes 46 seconds.
The horse's owners hired 600 boxers to protect themselves and the horse
in case of trouble. Six months later, again with Grimshaw in the saddle
and trained by Joseph Hayhoe, he won the 90th St Leger by three lengths
over 13 other horses. Gladiateur retired aged four and was put out to stud,
first in Kent and later in France (1869–1870). When France was invaded
at the start of the Franco-Prussian War he was returned to England for
his own safety. In January 1876, badly suffering from navicular disease,
he was put down. He was interred at Dunmow Stud Farm but his tail is
at the National Horseracing Museum in Newmarket.

FIRST

BELMONT STAKES

FIRST

FILLY TO WIN BELMONT STAKES

JEROME PARK RACETRACK, BATHGATE ESTATE, BRONX, NEW YORK, UNITED STATES OF AMERICA. WEDNESDAY 19 JUNE 1867.

The 230-acre Jerome Park Racetrack was opened on 25 September 1866 and attended by 20,000 fans including General Ulysses S. Grant, who would become president three years later. It was built by stock market speculator Leonard Jerome and financed by August Belmont Sr (1816–

DID YOU KNOW?

Jerome Park was named for Leonard Jerome who was born at Pompey, New York on 3 November 1817. He became a lawyer and a diplomat before making and losing several fortunes, earning him the nickname the "King of Wall Street". A keen sportsman, he helped with the organisation of the American Jockey Club on 9 February 1894. He was a significant investor in *The New York Times* for many years. On 5 April 1849, he married Clarissa Hall (1825–1895). They had four daughters. His second daughter, Jeanette, known as Jennie, was born on 9 January 1854. Aboard HMS *Ariadne* in Cowes harbour on 12 August 1873, aged 19, she met politician Lord Randolph Churchill (1849–1895), 23 and already going bald. In the British Embassy in Paris, she and Churchill were married on 15 April 1874. Seven months later in the cloakroom at Blenheim Palace, their son Winston Leonard Spencer Churchill was born. Leonard Jerome died at the age of 73 in Brighton on 3 March 1891.

1890) who would give his name to the race and course. The first race of the course's opening day was won by jockey Abe Hawkins. The year after the racecourse opened, the first Belmont Stakes was held and won by the filly Ruthless. Two dozen fillies have run in the Belmont Stakes and three have won. After Ruthless in 1867 came Tanya in 1905 and Rags to Riches in 2007. The Belmont Stakes was held at Jerome Park until 1890. On 10 June 1890, the Preakness and Belmont Stakes were held at the nearby Morris Park Racecourse.

On 4 October 1894, Jerome Park was shut to make way for a reservoir. On 4 May 1905, following the opening of the 430-acre Belmont Park, the race was moved there from Morris Park. Since 1926, the victor in the Belmont Stakes has received the August Belmont Trophy. From 1963 until 1967, the Belmont Stakes took place at Aqueduct Racetrack while repair work was undertaken at Belmont Park. At one and a half miles, the Belmont Stakes is the longest of any major race in the United States.

ONLY
GRAND NATIONAL HORSE DESTROYED BEFORE RACE BEGAN

CHIMNEY SWEEP, AINTREE RACECOURSE, ORMSKIRK ROAD, AINTREE, LIVERPOOL L9 5AS. WEDNESDAY 4 MARCH 1868.

Chimney Sweep was the 7/1 favourite to win the 30th Grand National. He was put down after running into a boulder marking the course before even one fence had been jumped. His injuries were so bad he had to be put down. The police fought a running battle with local "roughs". The race was won by The Lamb, ridden by George Ede under the pseudonym Mr Edwards, in ten minutes 30 seconds.

ONLY
GRAND NATIONAL-WINNING JOCKEY TO PLAY
FIRST-CLASS CRICKET

G.M. Ede, Hampshire CCC, Thursday 7 July 1864–1869; The Lamb, Aintree Racecourse, Ormskirk Road, Aintree, Liverpool L9 5AS. Wednesday 4 March 1868.

George Matthew Ede was born at Itchen, Southampton, Hampshire on 22 February 1834 and educated at Eton. He was a middle-order right-handed batsman and began appearing for Hampshire in 1861 before first-class cricket was recognised. In 1862, he scored the first century at the Antelope Ground, which would become Hampshire's first ground and also the home of Southampton FC from 1887 to 1896. Ede was one of the founding members of Hampshire CCC on 12 August 1863. He made his first-class debut in Hampshire's inaugural match in county cricket against Sussex on 7 July 1864. Hampshire (63/9 and 122) lost to Sussex (185 and 1/0) by ten wickets. Ede went on to play 15 first-class matches, scoring 257 runs with a top score of 52 (the first batsman to score a half-century for Hampshire) at an average of 9.51. His twin brother and nephew also played for Hampshire in first-class cricket. Ede, one of the top steeplechase amateur jockeys of Victorian times, rode 306 winners from September 1856 at Warwick Racecourse to 10 March 1870 at Aintree. Injured before the 1868 Grand National in a fall at Croydon Racecourse, Ede continued to race. On 10 March 1870, he took part in the Grand Sefton Steeplechase riding Chippenham. Ede fell at the Monument fence (now called The Chair) and, although he was uninjured, Chippenham staggered as he got to his feet and fell on the jockey, crushing his head and chest, breaking several ribs. Ede died aged 36 from his injuries three days later.

VICTORY FOR FRED ARCHER

Maid of Trent, Bangor Steeplechase, Bangor On Dee, Wrexham LL13 0DA Wales. 1869.

Fred Archer was born on 11 January 1857, in St George's Cottage, St George's Place, Cheltenham, the son of William Archer (1826–1867), a steeplechase jockey who won the Grand National in 1858 and who became landlord of the King's Arms, Prestbury, near Cheltenham. Both Fred's older brother, William (1853–1878), and his younger brother, Charles (1858–1922), were also jockeys. William died of injuries received in a fall in a hurdle race at Cheltenham riding Salvanie. When he was ten, Fred took part in a race between his pony and a rival donkey. He lost and went home in tears. He would always be a bad loser. On 10 February 1868, Archer became apprenticed to Matt Dawson, the Newmarket trainer based at Heath House. The contract included some unusual clauses. Archer "will not commit fornication nor contract matrimony … shall not play cards or dice tables … shall not haunt taverns nor playhouses". He would be paid seven guineas for the first year, nine guineas for the second, 11 guineas for the third and 13 guineas for the fourth and fifth plus "meat and drink" and a "hat and waistcoat each year and lodging during the said term". Archer was homesick and unhappy and asked his mother to rescue him. Gradually, his lot improved and he made his first public appearance in the saddle during Newmarket's second October meeting riding Honoria on 15 October 1869. He finished last. Soon after, he rode his first victor, the pony Maid of Trent in a steeplechase at Bangor. At the time Archer weighed just 4st 11lb.

JOCKEY TO WIN THE GRAND NATIONAL FIVE TIMES

George Stevens, Freetrader, Aintree Racecourse, Ormskirk Road, Aintree, Liverpool L9 5AS. Wednesday 27 February 1856; Emblem, Aintree Racecourse, Ormskirk Road, Aintree, Liverpool L9 5AS. Wednesday 11 March 1863; Emblematic, Aintree Racecourse, Ormskirk Road, Aintree, Liverpool L9 5AS. Wednesday 9 March 1864; The Colonel, Aintree Racecourse, Ormskirk Road, Aintree, Liverpool L9 5AS. Wednesday 3 March 1869; Aintree Racecourse, Ormskirk Road, Aintree, Liverpool L9 5AS. Wednesday 9 March 1870.

George Stevens was born at Cheltenham, Gloucestershire on 12 June 1833 and began riding when he was around 16 years old. From 1848 until 1870, he won 76 races. He won his first Grand National aboard Freetrader in 1856, beating 20 riders. Freetrader's owner W. Barnett gave him £500 (£57,000 at 2023 values) for the race. Stevens went on to win on Emblem (1863), Emblematic (1864) and The Colonel in 1869 in ten minutes 59 seconds and 1870 in ten minutes nine and a half seconds. He used the money from his wins aboard sisters Emblem and Emblematic to build his own home, Emblem Cottage. He died there on 2 June 1871, a day after he fractured his skull when his horse stumbled and threw him, while out riding and on his way home to his cottage.

ONLY
US TRIPLE CROWN RACE NAMED AFTER A HORSE SHOT BY ITS OWNER

Preakness, Preakness States, Pimlico Racecourse, 5201 Park Heights Avenue, Baltimore, Maryland 21215 United States of America. Tuesday 27 May 1873.

Preakness was foaled in 1867, the son of Lexington and Bay Leaf. On 25 October 1870, in a time of three minutes 47½ seconds, he won the first Dinner Party Stakes (later Dixie Stakes). Ridden by William Hayward Senior and trained by Charles H. Littlefield Senior, he outpaced the favourite Foster to take home the $11,000 prize. Preakness carried on racing until he was nine years old and in 39 starts won 18 races. On retirement, he was put out to stud and in 1875 sold to the 12th Duke of Hamilton (1845–1895) in England. Like many older men, Preakness became crotchety in old age and, one day in 1881, he refused to obey the Duke who shot him dead. Milton H. Sanford, his previous owner, donated the trophy he had won at the Dinner Party Stakes to a new race, the Preakness Stakes. First run on 27 May 1873, the inaugural race had seven starters. Survivor, a three-year-old, won the $2,050 purse by a winning margin of ten lengths.

ONLY
TRAINER RECEIVING A MEDAL FOR INTEGRITY
JAMES BINNIE, HAWICK MOOR RACECOURSE, HAWICK TD9 0PD SCOTLAND. 1873.

In 1873, James Binnie became the only trainer to be awarded a medal for integrity. The bosses of Hawick racecourse had a silver medal specially struck reading, "Presented to James Binnie by the stewards and committee for his long attendance and integrity in running horses at Hawick."

FIRST
FOREIGN WINNER OF BELMONT STAKES
SAXON, JEROME PARK RACETRACK, BATHGATE ESTATE, BRONX, NEW YORK, UNITED STATES OF AMERICA. SATURDAY 13 JUNE 1874.

Saxon was foaled in England in 1871, the son of Beadsman and Girasol. He was taken to America with Girasol and in 1873 won the August Stakes. In the summer of the following year, the brown stallion became the first foreign horse to win the Belmont Stakes – the eighth occasion it had been held. Ridden by George Barbee and trained by William Pryor,

Saxon won by a neck from Grinstead in two minutes and 39½ seconds. Of his eight races, Saxon won twice. He died in February 1895 at the Cliff Lawn Stud in Nashville, Tennessee.

FIRST
KENTUCKY DERBY

CHURCHILL DOWNS RACECOURSE, 700 CENTRAL AVENUE, LOUISVILLE, KENTUCKY 40208, UNITED STATES OF AMERICA. MONDAY 17 MAY 1875.

The Kentucky Derby is held annually on the first Saturday in May and is the first leg of the US Triple Crown (along with the Preakness Stakes (see 1873) and the Belmont Stakes (see 1867)). The race lasts just two minutes, the winning horse is garlanded in a blanket of roses and is the culmination of the fortnight-long Kentucky Derby Festival. The race was created by Colonel Meriwether Lewis Clark Jr, the grandson of William Clark of Lewis and Clark fame. Trips in 1872 to England and France inspired him to create the Louisville Jockey Club whose track became known as Churchill Downs after John and Henry Churchill, who provided the land for the course.

The first race was held on 17 May 1875 and 15 three-year-olds raced over one and a half miles (or 12 furlongs) before 10,000 people. In 1896, the race length was reduced to one and a quarter miles and has stayed that distance ever since. The first winner of the Kentucky Derby was Aristides, ridden by Oliver Lewis and trained by Ansel Williamson. Later the same year, Aristides, ridden by Lewis, came second in the Belmont Stakes. The race has become the oldest continuously held major sporting event in the United States. Since 1921, the University of Louisville Cardinal Marching Band performs Stephen Foster's 'My Old Kentucky Home' as the horses parade in front of the grandstand. In 1996, the race offered a $1 million purse which was doubled nine years later. The 2004 Kentucky Derby marked **the first occasion that jockeys sported corporate advertising logos on their clothing**.

ONLY

DERBY WINNER REPORTED TO

RETURN AS A GHOST

ONLY

HUNGARIAN-BRED HORSE

TO WIN THE DERBY

KISBER, EPSOM RACECOURSE, TATTENHAM CORNER ROAD, EPSOM,
SURREY KT18 5LQ. WEDNESDAY 31 MAY 1876.

Kisber was foaled in 1873, bred by the Hungarian Imperial Stud and trained by Joseph Hayhoe at Newmarket. There were 15 runners in the Derby; Kisber, a 4/1 second favourite, started quickly but jockey Charles Maidment pulled him back and the horse stayed near the back of the field. Kisber pulled into the straight in fifth place before putting in a spurt to challenge Petrarch, the favourite, when both mounts were a furlong from the finishing post. Kisber had the greater stamina and pulled ahead, winning by five lengths in two minutes 44 seconds, and took home a prize of £5,575. On 11 June 1876, he won the Grand Prix de Paris at Longchamp – the third of six horses to win both that race and the Derby. A crowd of 3,000, including the President of France, watched Kisber, the favourite, win by five lengths from The Oaks winner Enguerrande. The win took his earnings for 1876 to £11,173. That year, one of the most fashionable bonnets was named the Kisber. At the end of that season, he was retired and put out to stud. In 1886, he was sent to the Baltazzi brothers' stud at Napajedla, Moravia. In 1888, he joined a stud in Bad Harzburg in Germany where he lived out his days. He died in 1895 at Parhassy Castle but that was not the end of the story of Kisber. He was reported as having been seen ridden by a jockey in crimson, emerald and white (his racing colours) running at full speed around the castle – supposedly re-winning the Derby.

DID YOU KNOW?

Kisber's owners, Alexander and Hector Baltazzi, had financial difficulties and in the summer of 1876 were heavily in debt. They feared that creditors could seize Kisber in lieu of payment. However, they scraped together enough money to enter Kisber in the Derby. The prize money plus around £100,000 they won from betting on their horse eased their financial woes.

ONLY
GRAND NATIONAL
WITH FOUR BROTHERS RIDING

BEASLEY BROTHERS, AINTREE RACECOURSE, ORMSKIRK ROAD, AINTREE, LIVERPOOL L9 5AS. 2.58PM, FRIDAY 28 MARCH 1879.

In 1878, Tommy Beasley came second on Martha, losing by two lengths to Shifnal. In 1879, when the going was good to soft, he was back and again rode Martha although, at the second time of asking, he was placed third on the 50/1 horse. Willie Beasley guided Lord Marcus into eighth position. One behind was Harry Beasley on Turco. Johnny was aboard Victor II and pulled up immediately after Becher's Brook. Of the 18 jockeys taking part, nine were amateurs. The race was won by The Liberator ridden by Garrett Moore in ten minutes and 12 seconds.

FIRST
AMERICAN HORSE TO WIN THE DERBY

IROQUOIS, EPSOM RACECOURSE, TATTENHAM CORNER ROAD, EPSOM, SURREY KT18 5LQ. WEDNESDAY 1 JUNE 1881.

Fifteen horses took part in the Derby and Iroquois, ridden by Fred Archer and trained by Jacob Pincus at Newmarket, won by half a length in two minutes 50 seconds. When news of the victory reached America, dealing was suspended on Wall Street. Iroquois was foaled at Erdenheim Stud Farm, Pennsylvania in 1878, the son of Leamington and Maggie B.B. Her father was West Australian (see 1853). Iroquois stood 15½ hands or 5ft 1½ins tall. Archer was signed to ride Lord Falmouth's horses but asked for special dispensation to ride Iroquois in the Derby and this was granted. Archer had ridden the Derby winner, Bend Or, in 1880. On 14 September 1881, Archer rode Iroquois to victory in the St Leger, beating off the challenge of 13 horses. Earlier in the season, the horse came second in the 2000 Guineas on 4 May 1881 or he would have won the Triple Crown. In July 1883, he was sent back to America after he began bleeding from the nose exerting himself in races. In 1886, he was bought by Confederate General William Hicks Jackson and put out to stud at Belle Meade Farm near Nashville. Iroquois died aged 22 on 17 September 1899. The Iroquois Steeplechase has been held since 1941 in Nashville, Tennessee.

FIRST

MAN TO RIDE AND TRAIN A BELMONT STAKES WINNER

James G. Rowe Sr, Joe Daniels, Jerome Park Racetrack, Bathgate Estate, Bronx, New York, United States of America. Saturday 7 June 1873; George Kinney, Morris Park Racecourse, Bronx, New York, United States of America. Saturday 9 June 1883.

James Gordon Rowe was born sometime in 1857, somewhere around Richmond, Virginia. He began his racing career aged ten and by the age of 14 was regarded as the leading jockey in the US, a position he held in 1871, 1872 and 1873. It was in the last two years that he won the Belmont Stakes as a jockey – in 1872 on Joe Daniels (1869–1896) and in

1873 on Springbok (1870–1897). Joe Daniels, Springbok and the 1871 winner Harry Bassett (1868–1878) were all owned and trained by David McDaniel. Rowe retired from riding in 1875 when he hit 18 as he began putting on too much weight. He focused his efforts on training and on 17 May 1881 became the youngest trainer to win the Kentucky Derby, with Hindoo. Two years later, he trained the winner of the Belmont Stakes, George Kinney, and in 1884 was again triumphant with Panique. He went on to train eight winners, also triumphing in 1901, 1904, 1907, 1908, 1910 and 1913. He died of a heart attack at Saratoga Springs, New York on 2 August 1929, aged probably 72.

FIRST

HORSE TO COMPETE IN THE DERBY AND WIN THE GRAND NATIONAL

FIRST

HORSE TO WIN THE GRAND NATIONAL WITHOUT COMPETING IN A PREVIOUS YEAR

ONLY

GRAND NATIONAL-WINNING HORSE TO STAR ON THE WEST END STAGE

Voluptuary, Derby, Epsom Racecourse, Tattenham Corner Road, Epsom, Surrey KT18 5LQ. Wednesday 1 June 1881; Grand National, Aintree Racecourse, Ormskirk Road, Aintree, Liverpool L9 5AS. 3.15pm, Friday 28 March 1884.

Voluptuary was foaled in 1878, the son of Cremone and Miss Evelyn, at the Hampton Court Stud which belonged to Queen Victoria. The horse had a good pedigree. His father Cremone had won the Derby in 1872 and the Ascot Gold Cup in 1873. His mother Miss Evelyn (1866–1891) was the daughter of the 1844 Derby winner Orlando. Miss Evelyn's sister Julie was the mother of the Royal Hunt Cup and City and Suburban Handicap winner Julius Caesar. At the Hampton Court sale in 1879, Voluptuary – then called Battersea – was sold to Archibald Primrose, 5th Earl Rosebery for 660 guineas – the highest price received for a yearling.

The horse began racing on the Flat in September 1880, winning the Nursery Plate at Sandown Park. From the age of five, he ran as a steeplechaser and continued to race until he was 14. In 1881, he ran in the Derby which was won by Fred Archer on Iroquois. In October 1883 at the dispersal sale of Lord Rosebery's bloodstock, Voluptuary was sold for 150 guineas to H.F. Boyd. Five months later, he won the Grand National, ridden by Ted Wilson, seeing off Frigate by four lengths in front of a crowd of more than 100,000 in a time of ten minutes five seconds. When Voluptuary retired from racing, he began acting and was lauded for his performance in November 1898 as The Duke in the play *The Prodigal Daughter*. The play included a scene featuring a Grand National water jump. Like many actors, Voluptuary died in harness. He died, aged 24, in September 1902 performing in a Bradford version of the play.

FIRST
TURF RACECOURSE IN
UNITED STATES OF AMERICA
CONEY ISLAND JOCKEY CLUB, OCEAN AVENUE, SHEEPSHEAD BAY, BROOKLYN, NEW YORK, UNITED STATES OF AMERICA. THURSDAY 10 JUNE 1886.

The Coney Island Jockey Club was founded in 1879 and held its first day of racing on 19 June 1880. The first races were held on a dirt track. On 10 June 1884, the course played host to the first Suburban Handicap, created by James G.K. Lawrence, who became the track president. He went on to create the Futurity Stakes, first run on Labor Day (Monday 3 September) in 1888 – at the time the richest race in America. In June 1886, the club opened the first turf racecourse in America. It built the one-mile turf course inside the existing main dirt track replacing the Sheepshead Bay steeplechase course.

The first race was the Green Grass Stakes, a competition for three-year-olds over one and an eighth miles. It was won by Emory & Cotton's Dry Monopole. On 11 June 1908, Governor Charles Evans Hughes signed the Hart–Agnew bill that banned all betting at racetracks in the state of New York. Breaking the law could result in fines and up to 12 months in jail. Two years later, the law was strengthened to make the owners and directors of racetracks personally responsible for breaches. By 1911, all racetracks had shut. On 12 November 1914, the Sheepshead Bay Speedway Corporation was sold for $2,500,000 and the new owners used it for car racing. In December 1919, it was sold to property developers who knocked down the entire course and built houses. No trace of the track now exists.

━━●◆◆●━━

LAST
VICTORY FOR FRED ARCHER

BLANCHLAND, HOUGHTON STAKES, NEWMARKET RACECOURSE, CAMBRIDGE ROAD, NEWMARKET, SUFFOLK CB8 0TF. FRIDAY 29 OCTOBER 1886.

After a phenomenally successful career, Fred Archer's last victory was on Blanchland in the Houghton Stakes at Newmarket. It would be his 2,748th win from 8,004 mounts. His last race was on 4 November 1886 and he rode Tommy Tittlemouse in the Castle Plate at Lewes. He was unplaced. Throughout his career, Archer had battled keeping his weight down. At 5ft 9in or 10in, he was tall for a jockey and for breakfast he would eat half an orange and a teaspoon of castor oil. He also regularly dosed on "Archer's Mixture", a secret brew that when tried by someone else made them sick for a week. After his last race, Archer was burned out and returned home to Falmouth House in Newmarket. On 6 November, Archer was delirious. At 6pm that day, a doctor issued a bulletin stating, "Mr F Archer has returned home suffering from the effects of a severe chill, followed by a high fever." Archer was convinced that he had food in his stomach and wanted to take a purgative despite suffering from diarrhoea all night. He would not be dissuaded despite the advice of two doctors.

The next day, Sunday 7 November, Doctor John Rowland Wright returned to find that Archer's delirium had gone but now he was suffering from depression and was convinced that he was going to die. The following day, at 2.25pm, Archer was with his sister in his bedroom when he asked, "Are they coming?" They were his last words. He jumped out of bed and grabbed a pistol given to him by Thomas Roughton when his horse Sterling had won the Liverpool Cup. His sister, Emily Coleman, saw what he had done and rushed towards him. She tried to force the weapon from her brother's grip but "the revolver was in his left hand and I hurt my hand trying to push it away. He then threw his right hand around my neck and fired the revolver with his left hand. I saw him doing it but could not stop him, he seemed awfully strong." He had put the barrel of the gun in his mouth and fired. The bullet passed through the spinal column, severed the spinal cord and exited through the back of his head, a piece of bone still stuck to it. In October 1886, Archer had told his valet, Harry Sargent, to get the weapon repaired because of a spate of burglaries in the area. An inquest returned a verdict of "suicide during temporary insanity".

He was buried in Newmarket cemetery on 12 November, and left an estate valued at more than £66,000 (£10,975,000 at 2023 values). Archer's record of 246 winners in a season (1885) remained until 1933, when it was broken by Gordon Richards, on the anniversary of Archer's death.

FIRST
BLACK JOCKEY TO WIN
KENTUCKY DERBY THREE TIMES

FIRST
JOCKEY TO WIN SUCCESSIVE
KENTUCKY DERBIES

Isaac Murphy, Buchanan, Churchill Downs Racecourse,
700 Central Avenue, Louisville, Kentucky 40208, United
States of America. Friday 16 May 1884; Riley, Churchill
Downs Racecourse, 700 Central Avenue, Louisville,
Kentucky 40208, United States of America. Wednesday
14 May 1890; Kingman, Churchill Downs Racecourse, 700
Central Avenue, Louisville, Kentucky 40208, United States
of America. Wednesday 13 May 1891.

Isaac Burns Murphy was born on 6 January 1861 at Clark County,
Kentucky. Both his parents were slaves. His mother, America Murphy,
became a refugee in 1864, the year his father Jerry enlisted in the 114th
US Colored Troops at Camp Nelson, a Union Army depot to where his
mother had fled. After the death of his father, Murphy began his racing
career in 1875. He rode in the Kentucky Derby 11 times and won three
times. His first victory was in 1884 when he became **the only jockey
to have won the Kentucky Derby, the Kentucky Oaks, and the Clark
Handicap in the same year**.

In 1884 he won the first American Derby in Chicago, the most
prestigious race of the era; he won it again in 1885, 1886 and 1888. In
the 1884 Kentucky Derby, he rode Buchanan to victory in two minutes
40¼ seconds. In 1890, riding the Edward C. Corrigan-owned and
trained Riley Murphy, he won the race in two minutes 45 seconds. His
final victory came on Kingman in two minutes 52¼ seconds. In that

year, Murphy began to experience weight problems and his efforts to lose weight damaged his health. In 1895, he contracted pneumonia. On 16 February 1896, he died of heart failure in Lexington, Kentucky. He was a month past his 35th birthday. In 1955, he became **the first jockey to be inducted into the National Museum of Racing and Hall of Fame**.

ONLY

RECORDED INSTANCE OF JOCKEY READING HIS OWN OBITUARY

TOM BRUCKSHAW, SCOTLAND. 1892.

Tom Bruckshaw was a successful jockey, winning the Cesarewitch on King Lud in 1873 and riding 57 winners in 1876. Aged 39, he was riding Calyx at Musselburgh in Scotland when he had a bad fall. He was taken to hospital where doctors worked on him. He was surprised to read his own obituary on the first night in the local evening newspaper. He recovered but the fall necessitated his retirement in 1893 and he turned to training instead. He lived to be 90, dying on 14 November 1943.

FIRST

STARTING GATE
Ascot Racecourse, Victoria, Australia.
Friday 18 August 1893.

The first starting gate in the world was invented by J.L. Johnstone of Melbourne and was introduced to the sport in the winter of 1893.

LAST

MOUSTACHIOED
JOCKEY TO
WIN GRAND NATIONAL

David Campbell, The Soarer, Aintree Racecourse, Ormskirk Road, Aintree, Liverpool L9 5AS. Friday 27 March 1896.

David Campbell was born on 28 January 1869 and educated at Clifton College where he played cricket for the first XI. He moved to the Royal Military College, Sandhurst and on 15 March 1889 he was gazetted a second lieutenant in the 9th Queen's Royal Lancers. Campbell took up amateur racing in the Army and on 9 March 1894 he won the Maiden Steeplechase at the Grand Military Meeting at Sandown Park riding The Soarer, a horse he won on the toss of a coin. He sold The Soarer in early 1896 but still rode him in the Grand National. With two fences to jump, he took the lead and went on to win by one and a half lengths. Like many soldiers, he sported a handsome moustache – the last worn by a Grand National-winning jockey. He tried to repeat his success the following year again on The Soarer but he broke his collarbone falling at the jump after Becher's Brook on the second circuit.

He was promoted to captain on 3 May 1899. He fought in the Second Boer War and on 22 August 1902, he became a major. On 7 September 1914 at Moncel, he took part in the last "lance on lance" fighting in the war. He was discovered with "a revolver wound in his leg, a lance wound in his shoulder, and a sword wound in his arm". He was knighted in 1919, became Governor of Malta and resigned in 1936, dying not long after on 12 March.

ONLY

TRAINER "KILLED" BY A MEMBER OF THE ROYAL FAMILY

Mathew Dawson, Waterloo Lodge, Exning Road, Newmarket, Suffolk. 8pm, Thursday 18 August 1898.

Born at the family home Stamford Hall, Gullane, Haddingtonshire on 20 January 1820, Mathew was the second son of George Dawson. His father, elder brother, Thomas, and his younger brother, John, were all racehorse trainers. He served an apprenticeship under his father and in 1838 became head lad to Thomas at Middleham, North Yorkshire. Two years later, he was back in Scotland as a freelance trainer. He became a trainer at Newmarket at Heath House where the dukes of Newcastle, Portland and St Albans, the Marquis of Hastings and Lord Lascelles entrusted their horses to him. He trained horses for Lord Rosebery and won the Derby for the Prime Minister (see 1894). In 1891, he wanted to retire but kept working for Rosebery. Unable to walk properly because of chronic gout, Dawson won a further four Classics for Rosebery, including successive Derby winners in 1894 (Sir Visto) and 1895 (Ladas). He received special dispensation from the Jockey Club to take a carriage onto Newmarket Heath to supervise his horses. Between 1840 and his death, Dawson trained the winners of 28 British Classic Races, a record beaten by only two other men. In 1898, the Prince of Wales visited Dawson to whom he chatted. Dawson stood in a draught and was too polite to turn his back on the prince and ask for a window to be closed. Dawson, caught a chill and died at his home in Newmarket, aged 78. The times he lived were notorious for corruption in the sport but Dawson was above all the chicanery and had "a reputation which an archbishop might envy".

FIRST

FOREIGN CHAMPION JOCKEY

LESTER REIFF. 1900.

Fifty-four years after it was instigated, American Lester Reiff was the first foreigner to be named Champion Jockey. Lester Berchart Reiff was born on 26 April 1877 at Americus, Missouri, United States of America. Reiff began racing for trainer Enoch Wishard but, in late 1894, he was suspended for throwing races, a foretaste of things to come. In 1896, with his little brother John (1885–1974), he came to England to ride for expat Americans. The two brothers were clean-cut and small. In fact, John was so small that society ladies took to kissing him in the paddock. In July 1896, Lester Reiff was suspended by the Jockey Club for meddling with another horse during the Goodwood Cup and returned to the United States. In 1900, he returned to Britain, his licence having been restored and that year he rode 143 winners in 549 races, making him top jockey. In 1901, he won the Derby on the John Huggins-trained Volodyovski. The racing authorities began taking a look at the way he rode. After losing to his brother by a head on 27 September 1901 at Manchester, both Reiffs were reported to the Jockey Club, who ruled that they had not been trying to win and accused them of race-fixing. Lord Durham said the brothers were, with Enoch Wishard, part of a doping ring. The Jockey Club pulled Lester Reiff's licence. It was reinstated in 1904 but Lester did not return to the turf. He became an estate agent and venture capitalist. He died at Alameda on 10 October 1948. John Reiff was inducted into the US Racing Hall of Fame.

FIRST

DERBY WITH A
MECHANICAL STARTING GATE

Epsom Racecourse, Tattenham Corner Road, Epsom, Surrey KT18 5LQ. Wednesday 5 June 1901.

The first mechanical starting gate was used at the Derby in 1901 when Volodyovski (known to bookies and punters as "Bottle o' Whisky" because they could not pronounce his name) – ridden by American jockey Lester Reiff (see 1900) – was the 5/2 favourite for the Derby in a field of 25 runners, the biggest since 1867. It was a tight race and Volodyovski won by three-quarters of a length in two minutes 40.8 seconds, a new race record.

ONLY
GRAND NATIONAL WINNINGS USED TO REPAIR A CHURCH

SHANNON LASS, GRAND NATIONAL, AINTREE, LIVERPOOL. FRIDAY 21 MARCH 1902.

The 64th Grand National was won by three lengths by Shannon Lass, ridden by David Read and offered odds of 20/1. The going was heavy and Shannon Lass took 12 minutes three seconds to complete the course. Shannon Lass belonged to landowner and bookmaker Ambrose Gorham, who managed a stud farm and trained racehorses. He spent the prize money from the 1902 National on repairing the tenth-century church in Telscombe, Lewes, East Sussex. He died on 30 June 1933 and left his estate to Brighton Corporation with the proviso, "I direct the Corporation shall prefer a man who is a sportsman and not a total abstainer from alcohol and tobacco."

LAST
HORSE TO WIN 2000 GUINEAS AND 1000 GUINEAS

**Sceptre, 2000 Guineas, Rowley Mile Racecourse, Cambridge Road,
Newmarket, Suffolk CB8 0TF. Wednesday 30 April 1902; 1000
Guineas, Rowley Mile Racecourse, Cambridge Road, Newmarket,
Suffolk CB8 0TF. Friday 2 May 1902.**

Sceptre was foaled on 9 April 1899 at the 1st Duke of Westminster's
Eaton Stud in Cheshire, the daughter of Persimmon and Ornament.
Persimmon had won the Derby and St Leger in 1896 and the Eclipse
Stakes and Gold Cup in 1897. Nine days before 1900, the Duke died and
his bloodstock was auctioned. Robert Sievier bought Sceptre for 10,000
guineas. In 1902, she won the 2,000 Guineas in a record time of one
minute 39 seconds and two days later the 1,000 Guineas. That year she
became **the only racehorse to win four British Classic Races outright**.
She died in February 1926.

———•••—

FIRST
NON-BRITISH HORSE TO WIN
GRAND NATIONAL

MOIFAA, AINTREE RACECOURSE, ORMSKIRK
ROAD, AINTREE, LIVERPOOL L9 5AS. 3.34PM,
FRIDAY 25 MARCH 1904.

Moifaa was foaled in New Zealand in 1897, the son of Natator and
Denbigh. He began training and won nine of his 13 races and in June
1901 was sold by Alfred and Emily Ellingham to the sportsman Spencer
Gollan, who wanted to emulate the Prince of Wales (later HM King
Edward VII) and own a Grand National-winning mount. Gollan sent
Moifaa and three other horses, Toriki, Opea and Norton, to England
via steamship to train. Moifaa took time to settle in England and he was
unplaced in his first three races. Then he was entered for the 1904 Grand
National to be ridden by Arthur Birch. Moifaa started at 25/1. In the
race, Railoff was the first to go down, falling at the first, while Ambush

II, the King's horse, fell at the third. Moifaa took the lead at the fifth and never lost it. Moifaa jumped the last two fences perfectly to win by eight lengths from Kirkland with The Gunner a head away in third. The King watched the race from the Royal Enclosure and was so impressed with Moifaa that he bought the horse. In the 1905 Grand National Kirkland won the race and Moifaa fell at the 21st fence. Moifaa never ran another race and the King gave him to Colonel Brocklehurst, who went hunting on him in Leicestershire.

When the King died on 6 May 1910, Moifaa followed the gun carriage that carried His Majesty's coffin though the streets of London. The following year, on 3 February 1911, the winning jockey Arthur Birch died, aged 36, at Seville House, Victoria Drive, Eastbourne. On 6 December 1906, he had been racing on Black Ivory at Gatwick Racecourse when his mount fell. Birch got up but, as he did, another horse piled into him, breaking his back and leaving him confined to a wheelchair for the rest of his life. Birch left an estate worth £2,438 (£341,400 at 2023 values). On 11 January 1934, Spencer Gollan was run over by a bus and killed, five days after his 74th birthday, on Oxford Street, London.

DID YOU KNOW?

A story has arisen that Moifaa won the Grand National after surviving a shipwreck. The tale is not true. In January 1901, two ships set sail from Melbourne bound for England. One – the vessel carrying Moifaa and three other horses, Toriki, Opea and Norton – docked safely. The other, SS *Thermopylae* – carrying Chesney and Kiora – hit a reef at Table Bay off the Cape of Good Hope on the night of 12 January 1901. The crew swam to safety and alerted the authorities. One policeman rescued Chesney but could not find Kiora in the half-submerged ship. Ten hours later, locals found Kiora exhausted after swimming to a shallow reef on Mouille Point. He continued his journey to England and ran in the 1904, 1905 and 1906 Grand Nationals – falling at the fifth, third and eighth fences respectively.

ONLY

WELSH-TRAINED HORSE TO WIN GRAND NATIONAL

Kirkland, Aintree Racecourse, Ormskirk Road, Aintree, Liverpool
L9 5AS. 2.59pm, Friday 31 March 1905.

The 67th Grand National was attended by King Edward VII and a record crowd. It was won by Kirkland, the son of Kirkham and Perizonius Mare, and the only horse trained in Wales to win the steeplechase. It was his third and final participation in the race. In 1903, he came fourth and in 1904 he was second before his victory by three lengths in 1905. The jockey on all three occasions was Frank "Tich" Mason and in 1905 he was paid £300 (£78,000 at 2023 values) not to ride for a fortnight before the race so he would not get injured. Mason was Champion Jockey half a dozen times – in 1901 (58 winners), 1902 (67 winners), 1904 (54 winners), 1905 (73 winners), 1906 (58 winners) and 1907 (59 winners). Over the course of his career, he rode more than 720 winners although he only won the Grand National once. He died in 1969 at the age of 90.

ONLY

PRIME MINISTER TO OWN THREE DERBY WINNERS

Lord Rosebery, Ladas, Epsom Racecourse, Tattenham Corner Road, Epsom, Surrey KT18 5LQ. Wednesday 6 June 1894; Sir Visto, Epsom Racecourse, Tattenham Corner Road, Epsom, Surrey KT18 5LQ. Wednesday 29 May 1895; Cicero, Epsom Racecourse, Tattenham Corner Road, Epsom, Surrey KT18 5LQ. Wednesday 31 May 1905.

Old Etonian Archibald Philip Primrose, 5th Earl of Rosebery, 1st Earl of Midlothian, became well known in 1879 for his work on the first modern political campaign, the Midlothian campaign, of William Gladstone. Ten years later, he became the chairman of the London County Council. In 1885, he joined the Cabinet and on 5 March 1894 became Prime Minister, succeeding Gladstone. By this time, he was already a keen racehorse owner. Between 1875 and 1928 he won every major English race except the Gold Cup.

In 1891, his horse Ladas was foaled at the Crafton Stud in Buckinghamshire, the son of Hampton and Illuminata. He was trained by Mathew Dawson at Newmarket (see 1898) who had all but retired. Ridden by John Watts (1861–1902), Ladas won the Derby with the shortest-priced favourite in the race's history. His starting odds were 2/9 and there were seven competitors. Matchbox and Bullingdon made the early running but Bullingdon faltered around halfway, leaving Matchbox ahead in the home straight. But Ladas had inner reserves and overtook Matchbox; however, it was not over and Matchbox began to chase Ladas but the Prime Minister's horse held on to win by one and a half lengths with Reminder in third, six lengths behind Matchbox. Rosebery needed the police to help him escape from the scrum of admirers at the course. His win was cheered in Westminster.

Ladas was put out to stud and his children won 196 races. When he retired from being a stud, Ladas became extremely bad-tempered as he had "worn himself out with his restlessness and peevishness". He died at Mentmore, Buckinghamshire on 31 March 1914.

In 1895, Rosebery won the Derby for a second time and led the Liberals to defeat in the General Election (13 July–7 August) and stood down as party leader on 6 October 1896. His Derby-winning horse in 1895 was Sir Visto who was foaled in 1892, the son of the undefeated Irish champion Barcaldine and Vista. Ridden by Sam Loates, Sir Visto started in a field of 15 at odds of 9/1. Watching was the Prince of Wales, and Chibiabos took the lead before Beckhampton pushed forward and led towards the finishing post before, with two furlongs to race, Curzon and Kirkconnel moved ahead. Then with just 50 yards to run, Sir Visto took the lead and held on to win by three-quarters of a length from Curzon. On 11

September Sir Visto won the St Leger – it was his last victory. In 1896, as Rosebery stood down as Liberal leader, Sir Visto also retired and was put out to stud. Rosebery's final Derby winner was Cicero, foaled in 1902, the son of Gold Cup winner Cyllene and Gas, a half-sister of Ladas. In 1904, Cicero was the best English two-year-old, winning all five of the races in which he was entered. The following year, he was 4/11 to win the Derby, one of the shortest-priced successful favourites in the history of the race. Ridden by Danny Maher (1881–1916), the winning time of two minutes 39.6 seconds was a course record. Cicero retired in 1906 and became a stud horse. He was put down in 1923 after suffering an intestinal rupture.

DID YOU KNOW?

The Earl of Rosebery was educated at Eton (1860–1865) and Christ Church College, Oxford (January 1866–1869). At Oxford, he bought a horse he named Ladas despite this being against the rules. He was told that he had to sell the horse or leave the university – he chose the latter and left at Easter 1869. He told friends if he ever owned a horse he thought could win the Derby, he would call it Ladas. When the new Ladas won in 1894, Rosebery achieved an ambition he had formed at Oxford – to marry an heiress, become Prime Minister and own a Derby winner.

FIRST
RACE AT NEWBURY RACECOURSE

NEWBURY RACECOURSE, RACECOURSE ROAD, NEWBURY, BERKSHIRE RG14 7NZ. TUESDAY 26 TO WEDNESDAY 27 SEPTEMBER 1905.

The first meet at Newbury in its present location was held in late September 1905, a hundred years after the Newbury Races began at Enborne Heath. This two-day event moved to Woodhay Heath in 1811, where it stayed until 1815. It would be 90 years before regular racing returned to Newbury and even then it took the influence of King Edward VII for the Jockey Club to approve the new course. The Newbury Racecourse Company was founded in April 1904 and began building the course. It cost £57,240 (£8,283,000 at 2023 values). The first race, the Whatcombe Handicap, was won by Copper King, ridden by Charlie Trigg and trained by Charles Marnes. The jockey was given a gold mounted whip (value £10, £1,450 at 2023 values) while trainer Marnes was presented with a silver cup (value £25, £3,600 in 2023).

DID YOU KNOW?

During the First World War, Newbury Racecourse was used as a prisoner-of-war camp for Germans.

FIRST

FEMALE JOCKEY TO RIDE AGAINST MEN

DOROTHY TYLER, JOPLIN, MISSOURI, UNITED STATES OF AMERICA. 1907.

In 1907, Dorothy Tyler, 14, became the first female jockey to compete in a race against men. She rode her horse, Blackman, to victory in a race over a quarter of a mile. It was said of her in Joplin, where her father was the mayor, that "No boy of her age is her equal in physical strength."

ONLY

GRAND NATIONAL-WINNING HORSE TO TRAIN PULLING A TROLLEYBUS

RUBIO, AINTREE RACECOURSE, ORMSKIRK ROAD, AINTREE, LIVERPOOL L9 5AS. 3.03PM, FRIDAY 27 MARCH 1908.

Rubio was foaled at the Rancho del Paso stud in California in 1898, the son of Star Ruby and La Toquera. In 1899, he was sent to train in England but, in 1903, he suffered a serious injury. His owners took an orthodox view of his treatment and he was put to work pulling the trolleybus between the Prospect Arms Hotel and Towcester station. It worked and he went back into race training. His owner Major Frank Douglas-Pennant entered Rubio in the 1908 Grand National but the bookies did not rate his chances of success and he was given the odds of 66/1. The day was not helped by the weather conditions. A blanket of snow covered the course and the two dozen jockeys presented a petition to the Clerk of the Course demanding the race be postponed. He denied their request and the race went ahead. Ridden by Bryan Bletsoe (whose father had trained the 1901 winner Grudon), Rubio romped home by ten lengths. Fifteen of the 24 starters fell and Rubio became the longest-priced winner. The Lawyer finished a creditable third but died later that day. A post-mortem showed that he had only one lung, possibly the result of pneumonia in 1906. The following year, Rubio returned to defend his title but fell at the Water Jump and suffered another serious injury. He was retired after the race.

DID YOU KNOW?

After his success in 1908, Bletsoe took part in another half a dozen Grand Nationals but never again completed the course. In 1909, he rode Young Buck and fell off. Two years later, he suffered the same fate aboard Viz and he was also a faller on Blow Pipe in 1914. In 1919, after the First World War where he served in Egypt with the Northamptonshire Yeomanry, he pulled up on Irish Dragon and also pulled up on Glencorrig (1921) and fell at the sixth on Wavertree (1922). As well as the Aintree race, Bletsoe also won the Irish, Scottish, Welsh and South African nationals. He died at Northampton aged 84 on 16 January 1968.

ONLY
KING'S MISTRESS TO OWN
CESAREWITCH WINNERS

Lillie Langtry, Merman, Rowley Mile Racecourse, Cambridge Road, Newmarket, Suffolk CB8 0TF. Wednesday 13 October 1897; Yentoi, Rowley Mile Racecourse, Cambridge Road, Newmarket, Suffolk CB8 0TF. October 1908.

Lillie Langtry – known as the Jersey Lily – was an actress and socialite. She became the mistress of the Prince of Wales, later HM King Edward VII (see 1909) after sitting next to him at a dinner party on 24 May 1877. Both were married to other people at the time. Langtry's involvement with horse racing began in 1885 when she and her lover, the American Frederick Gebhard, purchased American horses to race in England. At 1.40am on 13 August 1888, a railway carriage containing 17 of their horses derailed at Shohola, Pennsylvania and burst into flames. One person and 14 horses perished.

The next year, she met George Alexander Baird, a wealthy bachelor, who gave her a horse named Milford. The rules of the time prevented them from registering horses in their names so Milford was listed as being owned by Mr Jersey. She and Baird began an affair which lasted until his death in March 1893. The year before, she had bought an Australian horse. Merman was foaled in 1892 at Hobartville Stud, Richmond, New South Wales, Australia, the son of 1880 Melbourne Cup winner Grand Flaneur and Seaweed. He became one of the best racehorses in Australian equine history. The start to his racing career was unimpressive – he lost his first, a six furlong one at Geelong Racecourse – but improved and won his third on 9 March 1895 at Flemington Racecourse, another over six furlongs. His last race in Australia came on 9 November 1895 when he beat Trentham in the Williamstown Cup. Merman's owner W.R. Wilson then sold him to Lillie Langtry for 1,600 guineas and Merman set sail for England from Melbourne on 3 December 1896 aboard the steamer *Aberdeen* (later part of the Ottoman Empire navy and torpedoed by the Royal Navy on 25 August 1915). Merman arrived in England in February

1897. In October 1897, Merman was listed at 100/7 for the Cesarewitch Stakes at Newmarket. He beat a largely foreign field, winning £40,000 for his owner. In 1900, Merman won the Gold Cup, ridden by Tod Sloan, before his retirement. In 2016 Merman was inducted to the Australian Racing Hall of Fame. In 1908, Langtry won the Cesarewitch for a second time, with Yentoi. In 1919, Langtry gave up her interests in racing and she died in Monaco at dawn on 12 February 1929.

FIRST
DERBY WINNER OWNED BY A
REIGNING MONARCH
MINORU, EPSOM RACECOURSE, TATTENHAM CORNER ROAD, EPSOM, SURREY KT18 5LQ. WEDNESDAY 26 MAY 1909.

Minoru, the third and **last horse to wear the colours of HM King Edward VII**, was foaled in 1906, the son of Cyllene and Mother Siegel. He began racing in June 1908 and from then until April 1910 he took part in 13 races and won seven times. In 1909, he won both the 2000 Guineas (ridden by Herbert Jones) and the Derby by a short head from Louviers. Minoru came close to capturing the Triple Crown but he was defeated by Bayardo in the St Leger, coming fourth of seven. Eye trouble forced Minoru to retire and he was put out to stud and soon after exported to Russia. It is claimed that Minoru and Aboyeur, who won the Derby in 1913, were seized by the Bolsheviks and executed as aristocrats. Louviers, the Derby runner-up, also suffered the same fate in Russia.

ONLY
ONE-EYED HORSE TO WIN
THE GRAND NATIONAL

GLENSIDE, AINTREE RACECOURSE, ORMSKIRK ROAD, AINTREE,
LIVERPOOL L9 5AS. 3.01PM, FRIDAY 24 MARCH 1911.

Twenty-six runners and riders lined up for the 73rd Grand National
with a record crowd in attendance; only 22 finished the course. There
are varying reports that the weather was either sunny or awash with
torrential rain. Film and pictures taken on the day tend to favour the first
weather forecast. Ridden by Jack Anthony, the one-eyed (he was blind in
the right) 20/1 Glenside took the lead when Caubeen (with G. Clancy
on board) and Rathnally (ridden by Robert Chadwick) collided after
Becher's Brook and got home by more than 20 lengths. Anthony was the
only jockey to complete the race who did not have to remount his horse.

ONLY
GREY FILLY TO WIN THE DERBY

TAGALIE, EPSOM RACECOURSE, TATTENHAM CORNER ROAD, EPSOM,
SURREY KT18 5LQ. WEDNESDAY 5 JUNE 1912.

Foaled in 1909, the daughter of Gold Cup winner Cyllene (he fathered
three other Derby winners) and Tagale, she ran her first race in October
1911. The following year, ridden by the American Johnny Reiff, she was
one of 20 horses to compete in the Derby. Watched by TM The King and
Queen, Tagalie was ranked 100/8. She showed her class by taking an early
lead and never surrendering it. She won by four lengths from Jaeger but was
never able to recapture that form. Tagalie died in 1920 after giving birth.

FIRST
HORSE TO WIN
SCOTTISH GRAND NATIONAL THREE TIMES

COUVREFEU II, BOGSIDE RACECOURSE, IRVINE, SCOTLAND. 1911;
BOGSIDE RACECOURSE, IRVINE, SCOTLAND. 1912; BOGSIDE
RACECOURSE, IRVINE, SCOTLAND. 1913.

Couvrefeu II was the first horse to win the Scottish Grand National three times, winning in consecutive years from 1911 to 1913. Couvrefeu II was the son of Curfew and Regime by Raeburn.

ONLY
SUFFRAGETTE TO DIE AT THE DERBY

EMILY WILDING DAVISON, EPSOM RACECOURSE, TATTENHAM CORNER ROAD, EPSOM, SURREY KT18 5LQ. WEDNESDAY 4 JUNE 1913.

In one of the most controversial moments in the history of the Derby, suffragette Emily Wilding Davison tried to grab the reins of HM King George V's horse Anmer as it went past Tattenham Corner. Davison was born on 11 October 1872 at Roxburgh House, 13 Vanbrugh Park Road West, Greenwich, south-east London. Her father fathered 13 children – nine by his first spouse and four by his 26-years-younger second wife. She was educated at Royal Holloway College, London and a term at St Hugh's Hall, Oxford (April–June 1895), but did not graduate because women were then not allowed to. She grew up to be a militant socialist and feminist joining Emmeline Pankhurst's Women's Social and Political Union (WSPU) in November 1906. She was arrested nine times (the first time in March 1909, for attacking a policeman), went on hunger strike on seven occasions and was force-fed by the authorities 49 times.

On one occasion when she was force-fed while in Strangeways, Labour MP Keir Hardie asked a question in the House of Commons and she was awarded 40 shillings (£285 in 2023 values) in compensation. To achieve her aim, she smashed windows, set pillar boxes alight (from December 1911) and planted bombs. Her activities resulted in her falling out with the WSPU.

She had a dozen letters espousing her cause published in the *Manchester Guardian* from 1909 until 1911. She was arrested on two occasions for attacking men she thought were David Lloyd George – one was a Cabinet minister, the other an innocent Baptist minister.

On 4 June 1913, she went to the offices of the WSPU, collected two flags in the union colours of purple, white and green and then caught a second-class train from Victoria to Epsom for the Derby. She took up a place at Tattenham Corner, the final bend before the home straight. As Anmer, ridden by Herbert Jones, approached at 35mph, she ducked under the barrier and four seconds later was hit by the horse. Anmer was brought down and landed on Jones. Davison was knocked out. Both jockey and protester were taken to Epsom Cottage Hospital. Davison never regained consciousness and died on 8 June 1913. She was 40 and a spinster. The race was watched by TM King George V and Queen Mary who had an equerry enquire over both patients. The King wrote in his diary that it was "a most regrettable and scandalous proceeding". The Queen, less sympathetically, called Davison a "horrible woman".

The Times reported, "She did not interfere with the race, but she nearly killed a jockey as well as herself – and she brought down a valuable horse … reckless fanaticism is not regarded [by the public] as a qualification for the franchise." The *Daily Mirror* – launched in 1903 as a paper for gentlewomen – wrote of the attendees, "It was quite evident that her condition was serious; otherwise many of the crowd would have fulfilled their evident desire to lynch her." The *Daily Express* said Davison was "a well-known malignant suffragette". Jockey Jones suffered a concussion and could recall little of the event. He said, "She seemed to clutch at my horse, and I felt it strike her." The inquest on 10 June at Epsom reported, "Miss Emily Wilding Davison died of fracture of the base of the skull, caused by being accidentally knocked down by a horse through wilfully rushing on to the racecourse on Epsom Downs during the progress of the race for the Derby; death was due to misadventure." She was buried on 14 June. Five thousand suffragettes followed her coffin and it was said 50,000 people lined the streets. She left an estate worth £186 1s 7d (£25,275, 2023).

DID YOU KNOW?

To add to the dramas of the race, the winner Craganour is **the only victor to be disqualified**. Aboyeur, ridden by Edwin Piper, took an early lead and kept it until he ran three horse widths to his left away from the inside rail. Other horses moved up to challenge including Craganour, ridden by Johnny Reiff. Craganour bumped Aboyeur who galloped towards the rail hindering Shogun, Louvois and Day Comet. Aboyeur bumped into Craganour and tried to bite him. Reiff and Piper encouraged their horses with their whips and the mounts bumped into each other several times. Craganour crossed the line first and his victory was announced to the crowd. Then the stewards launched an inquiry even though there had been no official complaint. After a long time, the stewards announced that Craganour had been disqualified and Aboyeur was the winner.

FIRST

RECORDED FILM
ABOUT HORSE RACING

Kissing Cup, *London. Monday 10 November 1913.*

In 1913, *Kissing Cup* was made. It is a 39-minute-long drama about a squire's jockey who escapes from a bunch of kidnappers and makes it to Sandown Park in time to win his race. It stars Harry Gilbey as Squire Heatherington, Chrissie White as Chrissie Heatherington, Cecil Mannering as Jack Heatherington, John MacAndrews as Ingham, the trainer, and Bobby Ingham as Arthur Ingham, the boy jockey.

FIRST

WOMAN TO OWN A
GRAND NATIONAL WINNER

Lady Nelson, Ally Sloper, Aintree Racecourse, Ormskirk Road, Aintree, Liverpool L9 5AS. 3.01pm, Friday 26 March 1915.

In 1914, Ally Sloper won the Stanley Steeplechase, making Margaret Nelson, the widow of Sir William Nelson, the first woman to own an Aintree winner. A year later, the lady and the horse returned to the racecourse for the only National during wartime. He won the race by two lengths despite the 100/8 odds. The victory did not appear assured as Ally Sloper landed on top of the second fence and jockey Jack Anthony only managed to stay aboard with the help of his brother, Ivor, who was riding Histon. Ally Sloper slipped at the Canal Turn and Anthony was left clinging to the horse's neck. The horse improved on the second circuit and, with many horses falling, made up ground and triumphed over Jacobus.

FIRST

FILLY TO WIN KENTUCKY DERBY

REGRET, CHURCHILL DOWNS RACECOURSE, 700 CENTRAL AVENUE, LOUISVILLE, KENTUCKY 40208, UNITED STATES OF AMERICA. SATURDAY 8 MAY 1915.

The 41st Kentucky Derby was the first to be won by a filly, Regret. Owned by Harry Payne Whitney (1872–1930) (the uncle of Dorothy Paget, see 1934) and ridden by Joe Notter (1890–1973), Regret came home in two minutes 5.04 seconds. Regret was foaled at Harry Payne Whitney's Brookdale Farm in Lincroft, New Jersey on 2 April 1914, the daughter of Broomstick out of Jersey Lightning. Regret was **the first horse to win all three Saratoga Race Course events for two-year-olds**:

the Saratoga Special Stakes, Sanford Stakes and Hopeful Stakes. The Kentucky Derby was her first race as a three-year-old and she was **the first unbeaten horse to win the Kentucky Derby**. From 1914 until 1917 she raced 11 times, winning nine and coming second once. She retired to Whitney's new farm in Lexington, Kentucky in 1917. She died on 11 April 1934 nine days after her 22nd birthday and was interred at the Lexington farm.

LAST

BLAYDON RACE

Stella Haughs, Newburn, Newcastle. 1916.

The first Blaydon horse races took place in 1861 on a circular island in the Tyne called Blaydon Island (Dent's Meadow). The day was such a huge triumph that they decided to hold the event again the next year, 9 June 1862. That day was immortalised in song by Gateshead-born Geordie Ridley (1835–1864), 'The Blaydon Races'. The horse races continued until 1865 and then began again in 1887. However, by this time construction work had been done on the Tyne, and Blaydon Island had gone. The racetrack was moved to Stella Haughs. The enthusiasm was gone, though, and allegations of race-fixing and a riot meant that the last Blaydon horse races took place in 1916.

FIRST

ENGLISH HORSE TO WIN KENTUCKY DERBY

FIRST

FOREIGN HORSE TO WIN KENTUCKY DERBY

OMAR KHAYYAM, CHURCHILL DOWNS RACECOURSE, 700 CENTRAL
AVENUE, LOUISVILLE, KENTUCKY 40208, UNITED STATES OF AMERICA.
SATURDAY 12 MAY 1917.

Ridden by Charles Borel (1883–1960), Omar Khayyam never had any
real competition in the Derby – the first English and first foreign horse
to win the race, in two minutes and four seconds. Omar Khayyam was
foaled in 1914, the son of Marco and Lisma and the great-grandson of the
first English Triple Crown champion, West Australian (see 1853). Omar
Khayyam began his racing career in 1916. The following year, his owner
had to choose between running him in the Kentucky Derby or Preakness
Stakes as they contested on the same day. Placed at 13/1, at one stage the
horse was in tenth place but put in a shift and beat the favourite, Ticket.
Just three weeks following the Kentucky Derby, Omar Khayyam was sold
to Canadian biscuit manufacturer Wilfrid Viau. In 1917 alone, he went on
to win the Brooklyn Derby, Kenner Stakes, Travers Stakes, Saratoga Cup,
the one-and-a-half-mile Lawrence Realization Stakes, Havre de Grace
Handicap and Pimlico Autumn Handicap. In 1920, Omar Khayyam was
put out to stud at Claiborne Farm in Paris, Kentucky. He died at the J.P.
Jones stud in Charlottesville, Virginia in 1938.

FIRST
WOMAN TO OWN A DERBY WINNER

LADY JAMES DOUGLAS, NEW DERBY, NEWMARKET RACECOURSE,
NEWMARKET, SUFFOLK CB8 0XE. TUESDAY 4 JUNE 1918.

Martha Lucy Hennessy was born in France in 1854, into the brewing
Hennessy family. On 4 September 1888, by now widowed from her cousin
Richard Hennessy (1835–1886) and the mother of four young children,
she married Lord James Douglas (born at 26 Wilton Crescent, London
SW1X 8SA on 25 May 1855; he had an elder twin sister, Florence,
who died on 7 November 1905), the fourth son of the 8th Marquess of

Queensberry and younger brother of the man who ruined Oscar Wilde's life. In May 1888, he had been imprisoned for contempt of court after refusing to stop harassing an ex-girlfriend whose mother had taken a restraining order against him.

By 1891, his drinking was out of control and his mental health was affected. He was summonsed to court for submitting a false census form but said he had left his wife and stepson to fill it in – and this unlikely excuse was accepted and the summons dropped. He committed suicide on 5 May 1891, cutting his throat at the Station Hotel, Euston. The coroner stated that he had killed himself while of unsound mind.

In 1910, his widow bought a house near Newbury and founded a stud farm there. Her most successful horse was Gainsborough (1915–1945), the horse that made her the first female owner of the race winner and also in 1918 won a Wartime-substitute Triple Crown triumphing in the 2000 Guineas and by three lengths in the 143rd St Leger (on 11 September 1918 held at the Cesarewitch course at Newmarket). The race was renamed the September Stakes as it was moved from Doncaster due to the First World War. Gainsborough became the 13th horse to complete the Triple Crown. Gainsborough was put out to stud in 1920 and was the leading sire in Great Britain and Ireland in 1932 and 1933. Failing health meant that Lady James sold her stud in 1940. She died on 31 January 1941.

FIRST

RACE BY MAN O' WAR

Belmont Park Racecourse, 2150 Hempstead Turnpike, Elmont, New York 11003 United States of America. Friday 6 June 1919.

Regarded by many as the greatest racehorse of all time, Man O' War was foaled on 29 March 1917 at Nursery Stud near Lexington, Kentucky, the second son of Fair Play (1905–1929) and Mahubah (1910–1931). He was bred by August Belmont Jr (1853–1924), whose father gave his name to the Belmont Stakes. Shortly after the horse was born, Belmont volunteered to serve in the United States Army in the First World War – he was 64 – and his wife, Eleanor (1879–1979) – named the foal Man O' War after him. The Belmonts sold Man O' War to Samuel D. Riddle for $5,000 ($108,320 at 2023 values) in the summer of 1918. At the start of his career, Man O' War was a feisty one. He would regularly throw his riders off. Riddle said, "He fought like a tiger. He screamed with rage and fought us so hard that it took several days before he could be handled with safety." Man O' War did have a strong relationship with Frank Loftus, his groom, and he taught Man O' War to fetch and to carry his hat. His debut race was over five furlongs and he won by six lengths.

FIRST
HORSE TO WIN US TRIPLE CROWN

Sir Barton, Kentucky Derby, Churchill Downs Racecourse, 700 Central Avenue, Louisville, Kentucky 40208, United States of America. Saturday 10 May 1919; Preakness Stakes, Pimlico Racecourse, 5201 Park Heights Avenue, Baltimore, Maryland 21215 United States of America. Wednesday 14 May 1919; Belmont Stakes, Belmont Park Racecourse, 2150 Hempstead Turnpike, Elmont, New York 11003 United States of America. Wednesday 11 June 1919.

Sir Barton was the first horse to win the US Triple Crown, although the name did not come into popular use until 1930. The journalist Charles Hatton created the term when Gallant Fox became the second horse to win all three races. Sir Barton, a chestnut colt, was foaled on 26 April 1916 at Hamburg Place Farm near Lexington, Kentucky, the son of Star Shoot (1898–1919) and Lady Sterling. His paternal grandsire was the 1893 English Triple Crown winner Isinglass.

In August 1918, Canadian businessman J.K.L. Ross (1876–1951) bought Sir Barton for a reported $10,000 but that year he developed blood poisoning after being kicked by another horse and was out of action for the rest of the year. In 1919, he was at his most successful. Ridden by Johnny Loftus (1895–1976), Sir Barton won the Kentucky Derby on 10 May from 11 other horses. He led from the off and won by five lengths. Just four days later, he won the Preakness Stakes again leading from the off and beating Eternal by four lengths. On 24 May, he won the Withers Stakes in New York and then 18 days later completed the American Triple Crown, winning the Belmont Stakes. In 1920, Sir Barton won five of his 12 races. He retired in 1921 and was put out to stud. Sir Barton died of colic on 30 October 1937, aged 21.

━━━◆•✦•◆━━━

FIRST
LE PRIX DE L'ARC DE TRIOMPHE

LONGCHAMP RACECOURSE, 2 ROUTE DES TRIBUNES, 75016 PARIS, FRANCE. SUNDAY 3 OCTOBER 1920.

French horse racing was governed by Le Société d'Encouragement and it arranged the major races. In 1863, it created the Grand Prix de Paris, a race to be run in July for the best three-year-olds from any country. The first winner was a British colt called The Ranger. In 1893, it widened the qualifying for horses with Le Prix du Conseil Municipal, which welcomed leading horses of different age groups. Run over one and a half miles every October, the weight carried by horses was based on previous outings. Its name was changed in 1974 to Le Prix du Conseil du Paris. At a committee meeting on 24 January 1920, a third major race was suggested. It was intended to be similar to Le Prix du Conseil Municipal but without any penalties for prior form. The committee decided to name the competition after the Arc de Triomphe, the site of a First World War victory parade by the Allies on 14 July – Bastille Day – 1919. The first

Prix de l'Arc de Triomphe was won in two minutes 39 seconds by a three-year-old colt called Comrade (1917–1928), ridden by Frank Bullock, trained by Peter Gilpin and owned by Evremond de Saint-Alary who won F150,000. The race was abandoned at the start of the Second World War in 1939 and 1940 but in 1943 and 1944 it was run at Le Tremblay.

DID YOU KNOW?

The owner of the horse that won the first Prix de l'Arc de Triomphe was Evremond de Saint-Alary (1868–1941), a scion of a prominent French West Indies family. He owned and bred many Thoroughbred racehorses. In fact, he was so dedicated to his horses that when a journalist wrote a piece criticising one of them, Saint-Alary challenged him to a duel.

FIRST

FILMED HORSE RACE

LAST

RACE BY MAN O' WAR

KENILWORTH PARK GOLD CUP, WINDSOR, ONTARIO, CANADA. TUESDAY 12 OCTOBER 1920.

Having won his previous 13 races, Man O' War's last race was in the Kenilworth Park Gold Cup in Ontario. The race was originally intended to be a competition between the three greatest horses of the age – Man O' War, Sir Barton and Exterminator. The distance of one and a quarter miles was too short for Exterminator and he was pulled from the race. Still, there was great interest and it was the first contest to be filmed in its entirety and later shown in cinemas. Man O' War pulled ahead of Sir Barton in the first furlong but both horses trailed two lengths behind Kummer down the back stretch. Man O' War quickened his pace and took a five-length lead. Keeping a steady speed, Man O' War won by seven lengths in two minutes three seconds. The time broke the track record by more than six seconds. The gold trophy was designed by the jewellers Tiffany & Co.

In a career lasting two years, Man O' War won 20 races out of 21 starts and set three world records, two American records and three track records. Put out to stud, Man O' War fathered 381 children. Perhaps unsurprisingly, in 1943 he suffered a heart attack and retired from his fatherly exertions. He died on 1 November 1947 after another coronary. NBC Radio broadcast his funeral live.

FIRST

RACE BY
SIR GORDON RICHARDS

CLOCKWORK, LINGFIELD RACECOURSE, RACECOURSE ROAD, LINGFIELD, SURREY RH7 6PQ. SATURDAY 16 OCTOBER 1920.

Gordon Richards was born on 5 May 1904 at Ivy Row, Donnington Wood, Oakengates, Shropshire, the fourth child and third son of the eight surviving children (four died) of coal miner Nathan Richards. After an unsatisfactory career as a junior clerk, he became an apprentice jockey after answering a newspaper advertisement. In 1920, Gordon Richards had his first ride. He was working at Jimmy White's stable in Wiltshire and they were playing another team at football. With the score at 3-3, a last-minute penalty was awarded. White told Richards if he scored he would give him a ride. Richards stepped up and put the ball in the back of the net. Not long after, he rode Clockwork at Lingfield. As with the football result, he came in fourth. His first victory would not come for another five months when he rode Gay Lord to victory at Leicester on 13 March 1921. He commented, "I can't remember ever being told how to ride. I just got on a pony's back and away I went." Four years later he won his first jockey championship, and between then and 1953 he missed the title only three times. In 1933, he won 12 consecutive races. A tubercular lung in 1926 meant he was hors de combat for a year and recovered in a Norfolk sanatorium. Richards was back in the saddle by the end of the year. From 1931 until 1953, Richards won 22 of the 23 jockey's championships – missing out on the 1941 title because of injury.

ONLY
GRAND NATIONAL JOCKEY ATTACKED
BY HORSE'S OWNER

AINTREE RACECOURSE, ORMSKIRK ROAD, AINTREE, LIVERPOOL L9 5AS. 3.04PM, FRIDAY 18 MARCH 1921.

The 80th Grand National was watched by TM King George V and Queen Mary, HRH the Prince of Wales, HRH Princess Mary and HRH Prince Henry. The race was won by the 100/9 Shaun Spadah – Irish-bred, Scottish-owned, English-trained by George Poole, ridden by Welshman Fred Rees. Rees was the only jockey to complete the race without falling off. There were 35 runners. The fourth-placed and last to finish was Turkey Buzzard – also 100/9 – ridden by Captain Geoffrey "Tuppy" Bennet, who fell off three times. He got back on and finished the race. Riding the horse into the paddock, he expected to receive congratulations from the owner, Mrs M. Hollins, but instead she was furious, believing he had mistreated the horse, and set about him with her handbag.

FIRST
HORSE TO WIN
LE PRIX DE L'ARC DE TRIOMPHE TWICE

Ksar, Longchamp Racecourse, 2 Route des Tribunes, 75016 Paris, France. Sunday 9 October 1921; Longchamp Racecourse, 2 Route des Tribunes 75016 Paris, France. Sunday 8 October 1922.

Ksar was bred by Evremond de Saint-Alary at his Haras de Saint Pair du Mont in Normandy in 1918. He was sold to horse owner and politician Edmond Blanc (1865–1920). When he died at Neuilly-sur-Seine, France on 12 December 1920, his widow took over ownership of Ksar. The horse's first win came in Le Prix de la Salamandre at Longchamp Racecourse on 19 September 1920. As a three-year-old, he was France's leading horse, coming first in five major races including Le Prix de l'Arc de Triomphe in 1921 in two minutes 34.8 seconds. He was ridden by George Stern (1882–1928). The following year, he was ridden by Frank Bullock who, two years earlier, rode Comrade, the first winner of Le Prix de l'Arc de Triomphe. Ksar's time in the second race was slightly slower, winning the race in two minutes 38.8 seconds. On both occasions, he was trained by Walter Walton. Just before he turned five, Ksar was retired after 11 wins and three places from 15 races. He was put out to stud and in 1935 sold to breeders in America, where he produced winning show-jumping horses. He died aged 19, in 1937.

FIRST
AMERICAN TO OWN A GRAND NATIONAL WINNER

Stephen Sanford, Aintree Racecourse, Ormskirk Road, Aintree, Liverpool L9 5AS. 3.01pm, Friday 23 March 1923.

Stephen Sanford was born on 14 September 1898 and educated at Yale University and the University of Cambridge. A successful polo player, he began fox hunting while at Cambridge. The 1923 Grand National was run in a thick mist. Sergeant Murphy, ridden by Captain Tuppy Bennet, a veterinary surgeon, won by three lengths, becoming the first American-owned horse to do so. Ten years later, he married the actress Mary Duncan after being introduced at a polo match by actress Marion

Davies, the mistress of newspaper tycoon William Randolph Hearst. In 1965, he suffered a stroke that left him wheelchair-bound until his death on 31 May 1977.

DID YOU KNOW?

There were two tragedies linked to the 1923 Grand National. On 27 December 1923, Captain G.H. "Tuppy" Murphy was riding Ardeen in the Oteley Handicap Chase at Wolverhampton when he fell and was kicked in the head by a horse. He died 17 days later without ever regaining consciousness. Following the death of Captain Murphy, crash helmets became compulsory for all steeplechases. On 17 April 1926, Sergeant Murphy had to be put down after suffering a broken leg at the Bogside meeting a few hours before the winner of that year's Grand National William Watkinson suffered fatal injuries in a fall (see 1926).

FIRST

BRITISH HORSE TO WIN
LE PRIX DE L'ARC DE TRIOMPHE

PARTH, LONGCHAMP RACECOURSE, 2 ROUTE DES TRIBUNES, 75016 PARIS, FRANCE. OCTOBER 1923.

Parth was foaled in 1920, the son of Polymelus and Willia, a daughter of William the Third, the Gold Cup winner in 1902. Parth was a member of the family that produced Mill Reef (see 1970, 1972). The Indian textile magnate Mathradas Goculdas sold Parth to King Macomber for 20,000 guineas. In 1923, Parth won, by a neck from Massine, the fourth Prix de l'Arc de Triomphe in two minutes 38.2 seconds. He was ridden by American Frank O'Neill (1886–1960) and trained by James Crawford at Ogbourne in Wiltshire. He started as a 35/4 outsider. Parth retired in May 1925 to spend his life at Macomber's stud farm in Normandy.

DID YOU KNOW?

The owner of the horse that won the fourth Prix de l'Arc de Triomphe was Abraham Kingsley Macomber (b. at Morristown, New Jersey, United States of America 7 March 1874). Known as King, in 1894 he set out for Africa where he spent six months exploring and surveying what would become Rhodesia. Macomber narrowly escaped with his life when the local Matabeles attacked the white visitors. He was then caught up in the Siege of Bulawayo where a small group of Britons and Americans fought off attacks for two months before the British Army arrived to rescue them. He went back home in December 1896. Three years later, Macomber married the heiress Myrtle Harkness and they became prominent figures in horse racing and breeding. When horse racing in America was shut down due to betting laws in 1911, Macomber moved his operation to England and France. As well as horse racing, he promoted tennis in Monte Carlo. A. Kingsley Macomber died on 6 October 1955, in Paris, France.

ONLY

PLOUGH HORSE TO WIN GRAND NATIONAL

AINTREE RACECOURSE, ORMSKIRK ROAD, AINTREE, LIVERPOOL L9 5AS. 3.08PM FRIDAY 28 MARCH 1924.

The 83rd Grand National was attended by HM King George V. There were 45 cameramen at the race – the most to have attended a sporting event at that time. Under a dusting of snow and frost-hardened ground, the race got off to a false start and it was delayed for almost eight minutes. By the Canal Turn on the second circuit, Winnal had a lead of 20 lengths but a loose horse impeded him and he refused. Eureka II and Mainsail also refused at the Canal Turn. Master Robert, a 25/1 joint-second favourite, ridden by jockey Bob Trudgill and trained by Aubrey Hastings for owner Lord Airlie, won by four lengths and took home the £5,000 (£389,000 at 2023 levels) prize.

Master Robert was regarded as too slow for racing and was sent to pull a plough on a farm instead. The farmer found he had too many horses and sold Master Robert for £50 and the horse eventually fell into the hands of Lord Airlie and Sidney Green, who sent him to be trained at Wroughton by Aubrey Hastings. It was discovered that he had a diseased bone in his foot and it took a lot of work by Swindon vet Frank Cumdell to get him fit once more. A week before the National, Master Robert went lame after a second place at Wolverhampton. He would never race again after Aintree.

Bob Trudgill was injured in a fall in the Stanley Chase on 27 March and ordered by a doctor not to race, advice that he ignored. He ended the race with blood seeping from a leg wound and he fainted in the weighing room. Fly Mask was second, Silvo (who had cost 10,500 guineas) third and Drifter fourth. The National was **the last race for Shaun Spadah** (winner of the 1921 National), at the age of 13. Post-race celebrations occurred at the Adelphi Hotel in Liverpool with 1,500 people present. Entertainment was provided by Bob Trudgill, who jumped over a model of Becher's Brook constructed from 20 magnums of champagne.

FIRST

KENTUCKY DERBY BROADCAST
LIVE ON WIRELESS

CHURCHILL DOWNS, 700 CENTRAL AVENUE, LOUISVILLE, KENTUCKY 40208, UNITED STATES OF AMERICA. SATURDAY 16 MAY 1925.

The Kentucky Derby was first broadcast live on the wireless 50 years after its first race. Listeners could tune in to WHAS and WGN in Chicago.

FIRST
AUSTRALIAN JOCKEY TO WIN GRAND NATIONAL

William Watkinson, Aintree Racecourse, Ormskirk Road, Aintree, Liverpool L9 5AS. 3pm, Friday 26 March 1926.

There was great US interest in the 1926 Grand National – the 85th running – which had 30 runners and riders. American Stephen Sanford had trained the 1923 winner and he had two horses three years later – Bright's Boy and Mount Etna. There was also 25/1 Jack Horner, who had finished seventh in 1925. The horse was trained by Harvey Leader for American owner Charles Schwartz, who had paid 5,000 guineas for him a week before the National. He was ridden by 40-year-old William Watkinson, who was born at Tasmania of Irish parents. He went to The Curragh as an apprentice to W.P. Cullen. In 1912, he relocated to Scotland and the stable of John McGuigan. In the 1921 Grand National, Watkinson, fell riding Blazers. In 1922, he had finished in second place by 12 lengths aboard Drifter. In 1923, on the same horse, he finished fifth. The next year, he fell on Fairy Hill II. In 1925, he was ninth on Drifter. In 1926, Silvo and Grecian Wave fell at the first fence and Lone Hand took the lead. Irish horse Knight of the Wilderness fell at the third while at Becher's, Lee Bridge fell and brought down Koko with him. On the second circuit of the race, Fred Gurney took Darraq into first place before Lone Hand fell at Becher's and broke his neck, necessitating him being put to sleep. Watkinson pushed forward on Jack Horner and the horse won by three lengths from Old Tay Bridge, who finished as runner-up for the second successive year. Bright's Boy was third and Sprig fourth. In 1927, Sprig went on to win the National under Ted Leader (see 1927). Jack Horner never ran again after the Grand National.

FIRST
GRAND NATIONAL BROADCAST LIVE BY BBC

AINTREE RACECOURSE, ORMSKIRK ROAD, AINTREE, LIVERPOOL L9 5AS. 3.04PM, FRIDAY 25 MARCH 1927.

The first Grand National broadcast by the BBC was in 1927. It was also the largest field to date with 37 runners and riders (40 were listed on the race card). The going was heavy and weather misty. The commentators were Meyrick Good and George Allison – the BBC's first sports commentator. The year 1927 was a busy time for Allison. On 23 April, he was at the old Wembley to commentate on the FA Cup Final for the BBC – the only time the trophy has left England and also the first FA Cup Final at which the hymn 'Abide With Me' was sung. Meyrick Good was the chief reporter for the *Sporting Life* and the author of several books. The race was won at his third attempt, in ten minutes 20⅔ seconds by Sprig – the fourth victor in five years trained at Newmarket. An 8/1 favourite, Sprig was trained by Tom Leader Jr and bred by Captain Richard Partridge of the Shropshire Yeomanry in 1917 while he was home from the trenches. He was determined to ride his horse in the Grand National once the Great War was over but it was not to be. On 28 September 1918, he was killed in action aged 42. His mother Mary sent Sprig to be trained by Tom Leader. His son, Ted (1903–1983), was entrusted with Sprig in the 1925 Grand National and he finished fourth. He finished in the same position in 1926, the year that Ted became Champion Jockey. Finally, in 1927, Ted, 24, rode Sprig to victory by a length from the 100/1 outsider Bovril III. In 1928, Sprig fell at the fifth fence and also fell in 1929.

FIRST
DERBY BROADCAST LIVE BY BBC

EPSOM RACECOURSE, TATTENHAM CORNER ROAD, EPSOM, SURREY KT18 5LQ. WEDNESDAY 1 JUNE 1927.

Sixty-eight days after the broadcast of the first Grand National on the wireless, the first Derby was aired by the BBC. There were 23 runners and the race was won by Call Boy, ridden by Charlie Elliott and trained by John E. Watts at Newmarket. The winning margin was two lengths with eight lengths between second and third. Call Boy won in two minutes 34.4 seconds.

FIRST
RACE BY PHAR LAP

RRC Nursery Handicap, Rosehill Gardens Racecourse, James Ruse Drive, Rosehill, New South Wales 2142 Australia. Saturday 23 February 1929.

Phar Lap was foaled at Seadown near Timaru, New Zealand on 4 October 1926, the son of Night Raid and Entreaty. His name means Sky Flash in Zhuang and Thai. He had a number of nicknames including "The Wonder Horse", "The Red Terror", "Big Red" and "Bobby". He was not the most physically prepossessing horse – he was gawky and his face was beset with warts. Hugh Telford bought him for 160 guineas for his brother, Harry, at the 1928 Trentham Yearling Sales. Hugh Telford, however, could not raise the funds and Phar Lap was sold to David J. Davis. His first race was a five-and-a-half-furlong handicap race and he came 13th and last. His first victory was the Maiden Juvenile Handicap at Rosehill on 27 April 1929, and he was ridden by 17-year-old apprentice Jack Baker. He began to improve and in the 1929–1930 season won 13 races including nine consecutive victories. His success annoyed certain elements and on the morning of 1 November 1930 some hoodlums tried to shoot the horse as he finished training. They were unsuccessful and that afternoon he won the Melbourne Stakes and on 4 November the Melbourne Cup from Second Wind and Shadow King. During the course of his career, he started 51 races and won 37.

FIRST

MAJOR RACE WITH TOTE BETTING

Newmarket July Course, Newmarket, Suffolk CB8 0XE; Carlisle Racecourse, Durdar Road, Carlisle, Cumbria CA2 4TS. Tuesday 2 July 1929.

On 27 April 1926, Winston Churchill, the Chancellor of the Exchequer, introduced his second Budget to the House of Commons and spoke for two hours. He announced that from 1 November 1926 there would be a tax on horse racing betting in Britain. Betting was legal at the time but the government wanted to put curbs on gambling that occurred away from the racecourses on places like street corners. He wrote, "It would be essential to prohibit any notice, placard, list of betting odds or other street sign which would flaunt itself before the passer-by … Do not suppose that I have in the slightest degree made up my mind on this proposal, about which I entertain the gravest doubts. I am afraid we might be accused … of having deliberately spread and multiplied the vice – I won't say vice, but evil?" Churchill believed that a two–three per cent levy on bets would raise around £3million (£235million at 2023 values) a year for the Treasury.

The unpopular tax was difficult to implement and the Home Secretary William Joynson-Hicks was opposed to it. Churchill twice had to cut the tax before abandoning it completely. Politicians do not like their ideas to be foiled either by their political opponents or public opinion. So in August 1928, the government passed the Racecourse Betting Act setting up the Racecourse Betting Control Board to regulate pool bets on racecourses. The idea was to provide a secure, state-controlled alternative to illegal off-course bookies.

The first major race meetings with Tote betting were the Flat race meetings at Newmarket (July Course) and Carlisle on 2 July 1929. **The first Tote-sponsored race** was the Tote Investors Cup at Kempton in 1956. In 1961, it became The Horserace Totalisator Board (the Tote) under the Betting Levy Act 1961. **The first Tote high-street betting shop** opened in 1972. In 1986, betting shops began to show live pictures from racecourses. In 1993, betting shops opened in the evening for the first time. In May 1995, Sunday racing began at Newmarket and Salisbury. In July 2011, the government sold the Tote to the bookmaker Betfred for £265m.

FIRST
TELEVISED DERBY

EPSOM RACECOURSE, TATTENHAM CORNER ROAD, EPSOM, SURREY KT18 5LQ. WEDNESDAY 3 JUNE 1931.

The Derby has been filmed since 1896. Broadcasting innovations began in the 1920s (see 1927) but before then one had to attend the event to see the excitement. In March 1930, the Baird Television Development Company began broadcasting regular sound-and-vision programmes during off-hours from its studio in London using the BBC's transmitters. After a successful experimental outside broadcast in Covent Garden on 8 May 1931, television's inventor John Logie Baird (1888–1946) said, "The fact that one was able to pick up the street scene showed that the idea of televising the Derby or cricketers at Lord's was not so fantastic as some imagined." Baird visited the Epsom racecourse on 6 May to recce the scene. A preliminary test was made of a minor race on 2 June. The results were rather disappointing – the pictures were quite blurry.

The next day Baird did not stay at Epsom for the race but returned to his offices at 133 Long Acre, London WC2E 9AA while his publicist Sydney Moseley stayed to do the commentary. A number of journalists went to Long Acre to watch the race on the BBC. The race was watchable but again was blurry because of interference. Baird publicly announced that he was satisfied with the transmission although it was at that time understandably more suited to broadcasting studio-based events rather than horse races. As future BBC chief engineer Thornton Howard "Tony" Bridgewater (1908–1997) put it, "If the horses stopped you'd only just know it was a horse but moving made all the difference … And, if it weren't for the commentary, you wouldn't have known which horses they were." Viewing figures were estimated at 5,000.

As for the race, it was won in two minutes 36.6 seconds by Cameronian, ridden by Freddie Fox, bred by the 1st Baron Dewar and trained by Fred Darling at Beckhampton. There were 25 runners and Cameronian won by three-quarters of a length.

LAST

RACE BY PHAR LAP

Agua Caliente Handicap, Agua Caliente Racetrack, Boulevard Agua Caliente 12027, Hipodromo, 22020 Tijuana, Baja California, Mexico. Sunday 20 March 1932.

Phar Lap's 51st and last race was the now-defunct ten-furlong Agua Caliente Handicap in Mexico which he won in track-record time despite splitting his hoof during the competition. He raced ten times in the 1931–1932 season and won nine of the races. Phar Lap died suddenly on 5 April 1932 at Atherton, California. His big heart (14lb compared to a typical horse with a 7.1lb heart) is on display at the National Museum of Australia, his hide at the Melbourne Museum and his skeleton at the Museum of New Zealand. His trainer Tommy Woodcock discovered Phar Lap in great pain and in a few hours the horse was dead from haemorrhages. A post-mortem examination showed his intestines and stomach were inflamed, leading to speculation that he had been poisoned.

In 2000, scientists declared that Phar Lap had probably died of duodenitis-proximal jejunitis, an acute bacterial gastroenteritis. However, six years later, boffins from Australian Synchrotron Research said that they were certain Phar Lap had been poisoned with arsenic on the orders of American gangsters who believed he could upset their crooked bookmaking. There is no evidence of any criminal interference.

In April 2008, it was revealed that Phar Lap was given potions to boost his performances and these elixirs consisted of arsenic, caffeine, cocaine and strychnine. Too much of this may have led to his death. An investigation, the details of which were released on 19 June 2008, showed that between 30 and 40 hours before his death, Phar Lap took a huge dose of arsenic.

The case continued to puzzle and on 31 October 2011 the *Sydney Morning Herald* ran a story based on an unearthed interview that Tommy Woodcock had given in 1936 in which he said he rarely gave Phar Lap any tonics. Retired New Zealand physicist Graeme Putt said, "Unless we are prepared to say that Tommy Woodcock was a downright liar, which even today, decades after the loveable and respected horseman's death, would ostracise us with the Australian racing public, we must accept him on his word. The ineluctable conclusion we are left with, whether we like it or not, is that Phar Lap's impeccable achievements here and overseas were utterly tonic, stimulant and drug free."

ONLY

HORSE TO WIN
GRAND NATIONAL AND CHELTENHAM
GOLD CUP IN SAME YEAR

Golden Miller, Cheltenham Gold Cup, Cheltenham Racecourse, Evesham Road, Cheltenham, Gloucestershire GL50 4SH. Tuesday 6 March 1934; Grand National, Aintree Racecourse, Ormskirk Road, Aintree, Liverpool L9 5AS. Friday 23 March 1934.

Golden Miller was foaled at Pelletstown, County Meath, Ireland in 1927, the son of Goldcourt (b. 1913) and Miller's Pride (b. 1909). Goldcourt never raced but two of his offspring won the Irish Grand National. Golden Miller was sold several times before he was bought by Dorothy Paget, who had hired one of his former owners, Basil Briscoe, as her private trainer. In February 1931, Golden Miller made his first appearance in a steeplechase at Newbury and won but he was disqualified for carrying the wrong weight. He ran in the Cheltenham Gold Cup for the first time on 1 March 1932 and won.

He retained his title on 7 March 1933 by ten lengths when he was ridden by Billy Stott. On 6 March 1934, he won, ridden by Gerry Wilson, in six minutes 30 seconds. On 14 March 1935, again ridden by Gerry Wilson, he won by three-quarters of a length, and on 12 March 1936, ridden by Evan Williams, he won by 12 lengths from Royal Mail, ridden by Fulke Walwyn.

There was no race in 1931 because of frost or 1937 due to flooding. On 10 March 1938, he came second to Morse Code, beaten by two lengths. In November 1933, Golden Miller won at Lingfield, beating Thomond II with Gerry Wilson on board. Golden Miller started at 6/5 in the Gold Cup in early March. Thomond II did not run but Golden Miller was challenged by El Hadjar and Kellsboro' Jack with three fences to go. However, El Hadjar fell and Kellsboro' Jack could not maintain his pace and Golden Miller won by six lengths from Avenger.

Seventeen days later, Golden Miller was at Aintree but with no Kellsboro' Jack (the 1933 Grand National winner) to challenge him.

Wilson kept Golden Miller towards the back of the 30-strong field. Then towards the end of the first circuit, he pushed the horse forward and as they crossed Melling Road for the second time, Golden Miller moved up to be equal first with Delaneige but it was not until the final fence that Wilson gave his horse his head and Golden Miller romped home by five lengths despite carrying 12st 2lb in a new record time of nine minutes 20.4 seconds. Even though it was regarded as the best performance of his career, Golden Miller did not like Aintree. He ran five times but only completed the course once. In one race, he was knocked over at the first but the other three, he refused at the open ditch approaching the 11th. Author Roger Mortimer wrote of the horse, "It took some little time for the racing public to accept Golden Miller as the great horse that he was because he lacked the almost insolent panache of Easter Hero. In a race he was inclined to be idle, while his jumping was quick and economical rather than brilliantly spectacular. He was accustomed to jump off his forehand and was therefore not the ideal horse for Aintree. His class and cleverness, combined with courage and stamina, earned him one Grand National, but in fact he was essentially a park course type. Cheltenham was a track that suited him to perfection, his long stride and apparently boundless stamina earning a rich dividend in that stiff uphill climb to the winning post." Golden Miller retired in 1939, having won 29 times in 52 races. He was put to sleep in 1957 after suffering a heart attack. He is interred at Elsenham Stud, Elsenham, west Essex.

DID YOU KNOW?

Dorothy Paget was the British Flat racing Champion Owner in 1943, and the leading National Hunt owner in 1933–1934, 1940–1941 and 1951–1952. She was also one of the most eccentric figures in any sport. The Honourable Dorothy Wyndham Paget was born at 32 Green Street, Mayfair, London W1K 7AU (later the Brazilian Embassy) on 21 February 1905, the second daughter and youngest child of Almeric Paget, later the 1st Baron Queenborough (1861–1949) and Pauline

Payne Whitney (1874–1916), the eldest daughter of the wealthy American politician – he was the Secretary of the Navy – William C. Whitney. She was close to her mother and was devastated when Lady Queenborough died, aged 42, when her daughter was 11. Spoiled as a child, servants never corrected her – she was so badly behaved that she was expelled from six schools. Her behaviour worsened. DP, as she was known, used her not inconsiderable wealth to fund motor racing, show jumping and horse racing.

Her horses won 1,532 races including seven Cheltenham Gold Cups, two Champion Hurdles, a Grand National and a wartime Derby (in 1943). She was not a financial success on the racecourses, losing more than £3 million. She would also spend a fortune on bets. Spending her days in bed, she rose at night, ate breakfast at 8.30pm and dined at 7am, and put bets on races that had already happened. She swore to the bookies that she did not know the result and since many of the horses she chose had already lost, they were happy to believe her and pay out on the rare occasions she "picked" a winner. Her household staff all had different-coloured uniforms (apart from green which she hated) and she would address them by their colour rather than their names. She was standoffish, ineffably rude and wore a speckled blue tweed coat to cover her 20-stone body. She did not care what the racegoers thought of her as "the public don't pay my training bills" and proclaimed herself as an ardent Conservative "because I dislike being ruled by the lower classes". When she caught a train, she would hire a railway compartment so she would have privacy and always bought two seats at the theatre or Wimbledon, one for her and one for her handbag. She disliked men and claimed that she was sometimes physically sick in their presence. She told her cousin, May Snow, one of the few family members with whom she got on, that the worst experience of her life was being kissed by a slightly drunk, middle-aged Frenchman in Claridge's Hotel on the Champs Elysées. "I rushed to the loo and threw up," she said. Unsurprisingly, she remained a spinster. When she congratulated Golden Miller, it was said that this was the first time she had ever kissed a male although a wag noted that he was a gelding.

Following her nocturnal schedule, at 4.30am on 9 February 1960 at her home, Hermits Wood Lodge, Nightingales Lane, Chalfont St Giles, Chiltern, Buckinghamshire HP8 4SJ, she was looking at a racing calendar for Wetherby. Sixty minutes later, she was found dead from heart failure, no doubt caused by her obesity and 100-cigarettes-a-day habit. She was 12 days short of her 55th birthday. Her estate was valued at £3,803,380 (£112,068,145 at 2023 values) (reduced by duties to £736,000, a still not unhealthy £21,686,540, 2023).

LAST
USE OF RATTLES IN HORSE RACING

Speed On, Folkestone Racecourse, Stone Street, Westenhanger, Hythe, Kent CT21 4HY Kent. August 1935.

When the jockey J. Hickey won on Speed On at a meet at Folkestone he used an unusual form of encouragement. Urged on by the trainer H. Hedges, Hickey used a rattle to inspire the horse. The stewards at Folkestone were uncertain of the legality of using such an action and sent the case upstairs to the Jockey Club, who deemed the rattle unsporting and banned it on 30 August 1935.

FIRST
US-BRED HORSE TO WIN GRAND NATIONAL

ONLY
HORSE TO WIN GRAND NATIONAL AND AMERICAN GRAND NATIONAL

Battleship, American Grand National, Belmont Park, 2150 Hempstead Turnpike, Elmont, New York 11003 United States of America. 1934;

Grand National, Aintree Racecourse, Ormskirk Road, Aintree, Liverpool
L9 5AS. Friday 25 March 1938.

Battleship was foaled in 1927, the son of Man O' War (see 1919, 1920)
and Quarantine and was originally intended for Flat racing. Sold in
1931, Battleship was turned into a steeplechaser and took part over the
jumps two years later. The following year, he won the American Grand
National, ridden by Carroll K. Bassett, with a victory over Arc Light.
In July 1936, Battleship was sent to England, where he was under the
tutelage of Reg Hobbs for the 1937 Grand National. Hobbs decided not
to enter Battleship for 1937 but entered him in the 1938 Aintree race.

That year, Battleship, a 40/1 outsider, was ridden by Hobbs's 17-year-
old son Bruce (1920–2005). It rained intermittently on the morning of
the race and the weather was described as cold and disagreeable but the
sun came out in time for the race. The crowd was estimated at 250,000
or more. There were 36 starters. At the Water Jump (the 16th fence),
the only Canadian-owned starter, the Kentucky-bred Rock Lad, owned
by H.R. Bain of Toronto and ridden by Jack Bissill, fell and broke his
back, dying almost immediately. Two fences from home, Royal Danieli
was about a length ahead of Workman, and Battleship was just behind.
Then Workman began to tire and Battleship went forward, challenging
Royal Danieli. At the final jump, Royal Danieli led slightly but Battleship
refused to give in and won the 97th Grand National by a head in a photo
finish from Royal Danieli in nine minutes, 29.8 seconds. Ten lengths back
in third place was Workman, and five lengths behind him was James B.
Rank's Cooleen. The order of the others who finished was Delachance,
Red Knight II, Blue Shirt, Hopeful Hero, Underbid, Bachelor Prince,
Lough Cottage, Provocative and Drim. As is frequently the case in
the National, a riderless horse (Takvor Pacha who fell at the sixth) had
preceded the winner across the finish line. Hobbs said, "I didn't hit the
little horse because he wouldn't go for the stick, but he gave everything and
got up and won. I thought it was half a length but they gave it as a head
and all the Irish said if there was a photograph I would have been second."

Three months after his Grand National triumph, Battleship returned to New York where he was met by a crowd including Mayor Fiorello LaGuardia and the actor Randolph Scott (the husband of the owner). Battleship was put out to stud where he sired Sea Legs, the winner of the 1952 American Grand National. Battleship died in 1958 at the age of 31. As for Bruce Hobbs, in 1938 he was **the first jockey to win three Grand Nationals in one year** – the Aintree one, the American and Long Island's Cedarhurst. That year he also had a fall in which he broke his spine. Despite being advised that his riding days were over, he got back in the saddle but retired aged 25 to become a trainer.

━━•◆◆•━━

LAST
RACE BY SEABISCUIT

Santa Anita Handicap, Santa Anita Park, 285 West Huntington Drive, Arcadia, California 91007 United States of America. Saturday 2 March 1940.

After heavy rainfall, the sun finally peaked through the clouds at Santa Anita on 29 February 1940. That week the National Weather Service had been swamped by calls from people wanting to know if the rain would abate by the time of Seabiscuit's last race. When the rain did stop, 50 workers were out on the course with a heavy roller and sponging the mud out of puddles. Fans began gathering before dawn and soon the car park was full to bursting. The gates were opened at 10am and 5,000 people rushed into the clubhouse and grandstand. The grandstand was full by 10.30am and the car park could take no more by midday. A priest from across the street opened his churchyard to accommodate more cars. Still people arrived, causing traffic chaos. Celebrities including Clark Gable and Carole Lombard, Sonja Henie, Jack Benny, Bing Crosby and James Stewart were among the 78,000 people who packed the stands albeit the famous were in private boxes.

Johnny "Red" Pollard (1909–1981) mounted Seabiscuit and led him to the starting gate. The bell rang and the gates opened. Whichcee took the lead but Pollard kept Seabiscuit about half a length in arrears then Wedding Call came up from behind and bumped into Seabiscuit, sending him towards the rail. Seabiscuit was caught behind the two horses, apparently without a way through. Seabiscuit was carrying 130lb, ten more than Whichcee and 22lb more than Wedding Call. Then the two horses in front moved left and right and Pollard seized the opportunity and urged his mount forward. Seabiscuit moved ahead into the home stretch. Just when it seemed he was clear, Kayak pulled into the lead. Pollard asked his mount for one more burst of acceleration and Seabiscuit lurched forward. The horse romped home in two minutes one and a fifth seconds.

━━•◆•◆•━━

FIRST

GRAND NATIONAL-WINNING JOCKEY TO DIE IN SECOND WORLD WAR

TOMMY CULLINAN, OXFORD. THURSDAY 11 APRIL 1940.

Thomas Brady Cullinan was born in Ennis, County Clare, Ireland on 15 May 1906. He began as an amateur jockey in 1923 and in 1927 became champion amateur. He travelled to England that year and turned professional in January 1928. On 30 March 1928, he came second in the Grand National aboard Billy Barton. All the horses fell apart from two and even Billy Barton fell at the 30th before Cullinan remounted to finish the race. The 1928 race set the record for the fewest finishers in a Grand National. In April 1928, he won the Irish Grand National on Don Sancho. Two years later, he was the winning jockey in the 1930 Grand National – the 89th running – when he rode the 100/8 outsider Shaun Goilin. The name means John the Fairy in English and Cullinan said, "I think there must be something of a Fairy about him, judging by the way he carried me to victory at Liverpool. He gave me a most marvellous ride." There were 41 horses running that day and all survived the race apart from Derby Day, who fell at the fourth and had to be destroyed.

That year (1930), he achieved the treble of the National, the Cheltenham Gold Cup on Easter Hero and the Champion Hurdle on Brown Tony. Ten years later, Gunner Cullinan was serving with 90 Battery, 35 Light Anti-Aircraft Regiment of the Royal Artillery at an RAF station in Oxford. It was reported that returning to base after a night on the town in the spring of 1940, he was shot dead, aged 33, by a nervous sentry. In fact, Cullinan committed suicide during a fit of depression. He was buried in Swindon, Wiltshire.

DID YOU KNOW?

Three other Grand National-winning jockeys also died during the conflict. Frank Furlong (Reynoldstown, 1935: killed, aged 32, in an air crash on 13 September 1944); Bobby Everett (Gregalach, 1929: killed, aged 40, on 26 January 1942 when his Hurricane crashed on the beach in Llanddona in Anglesey, Wales) and Flight Sergeant Mervyn Jones (Bogskar, 1940 – the last National of the war years: died, aged 22, in April 1942 when his Spitfire was shot down after a sortie over Norway when he was attached to Bomber Command).

LAST
MEET AT GATWICK RACECOURSE

**GATWICK RACECOURSE, NEAR HORLEY, SURREY.
SATURDAY 15 JUNE 1940.**

In 1826, Croydon Racecourse opened but eventually weather and badly behaved crowds meant the venue was unpopular. In 1890, the county council announced that they would not be renewing the racecourse's licence after the last meeting on 15 October 1890. In May 1890, the New Croydon Racecourse Committee announced they were looking for a new site and would leave by December. The committee purchased a large section of the Gatwick Estate to turn it into a new course and stables for 500 horses. The Jockey Club rejected the application to hold Flat racing on the new site in July 1890 but then changed the decision. The licence was transferred from Croydon to Gatwick and in November 1890 Mr Stevens, of East Grinstead, was given a contract to build a new iron and wood grandstand at Gatwick. The cost was £10,500 (£1,726,237 at 2023 values). The London, Brighton and South Coast Railway Company agreed to build a new station with a direct service from London in less than an hour.

John Farlow sold the old Manor of Gatwick on 13 December 1890 and Gatwick Racecourse opened on 7 October 1891. Its main track was an oval of a mile and seven furlongs. The *Sporting Life* reported, "Considering the persistent rain of Tuesday and the overnight prospects of more rain, under the circumstances the inaugural meeting at Gatwick was more favourable than could have been anticipated. Although the morning was unpropitious, the weather cleared up by noon, and no rain fell during racing. The opening of the new course resembles much the first night of a play, when absolute readiness can only be achieved by practice. A few small details were overlooked, some of the new machinery did not work, but there was not much with which to find fault with the Gatwick administrators. Everyone admired the actual racecourse and its surroundings, with the enclosure voted as the prettiest seen by any racegoer. What it will be like on a glorious summer day must be left to the imagination; music, flowers, delicious promenades and everything to please is so closely associated with our noble pastime as to make one think that, in spite of a good opening, there may be still better days to come." During the First World War, the Grand National was run at Gatwick three times because the War Office took over Aintree.

On 24 March 1916, the Grand National – called the Racecourse Association Steeplechase – saw Vermouth, ridden by Jack Reardon, beat Irish Mail and Schoolmoney. The next year on 21 March 1917, the War Steeplechase was won by Ballymacad, beating Chang and Ally Sloper. The third and final time was on 21 March 1918, also the War Steeplechase, when Poethlyn was ridden to victory by Ernest Piggott, the grandfather of Lester Piggott. In 1939, as the clouds of war began to gather over Europe, it seemed likely that the racecourse would be taken over by the military. The last National Hunt meeting took place on 27 and 28 March 1940. The final Flat race meeting took place on 14 and 15 June 1940. On 6 June 1936, Gatwick Airport had been officially reopened by Lord Swinton, the Secretary of State for Air, and the airport was officially decommissioned on 31 August 1946. The revamped airport was officially opened by HM Queen Elizabeth II on 9 June 1958. The airport was expanded onto the site of the course and there is no evidence a racecourse ever existed.

ONLY

TRAVERS STAKES GRAND SLAM WINNER

Whirlaway, Kentucky Derby, Churchill Downs Racecourse, 700 Central Avenue, Louisville, Kentucky 40208 United States of America. Saturday 3 May 1941; Preakness Stakes, Pimlico Racecourse, 5201 Park Heights Avenue, Baltimore, Maryland 21215 United States of America. Saturday 31 May 1941; Belmont Stakes, Belmont Park Racecourse, 2150 Hempstead Turnpike, Elmont, New York 11003 United States of America. Saturday 7 June 1941; Travers Stakes, Saratoga Race Course, 267 Union Avenue, Saratoga Springs, New York 12866 United States of America. Saturday 16 August 1941.

There are two ways to win the Quadruple Crown in American racing. One is to win the Triple Crown and then the Travers Stakes and the other is the Triple Crown followed by the Breeders' Cup Classic. Only one horse has achieved each. The first was Whirlaway in 1941 and the second was American Pharoah (see 2015). Whirlaway was sired by English Derby winner Blenheim, out of Dustwhirl, on 2 April 1938 at Calumet Farm in Lexington, Kentucky. Trained by Ben A. Jones and ridden by Eddie Arcaro (1916–1997), Whirlaway won the Kentucky Derby in two minutes one and two fifths of a second by eight lengths.

A few weeks later, Whirlaway triumphed in the Preakness Stakes. The following week was the 73rd running of the Belmont Stakes and there were just four horses competing. With half a mile gone, Arcaro pushed Whirlaway to the front. He remembered, "I was last with Whirlaway going away and I was going to stay last for a while. But at the mile post, there was no pace. It was very slow. So I yelled to those other jocks: 'I'm leaving.'" Through the back stretch Whirlaway opened up a lead of six or eight lengths. Robert Morris (ridden by Aberdonian Alfred Robertson), Itabo and Yankee Chance followed. Whirlaway beat Robert Morris by two and a half lengths to become the fifth Triple Crown champion, before a crowd of 30,801 people on the final afternoon of a record-breaking Belmont Park meeting.

Whirlaway's owner Warren Wright had to choose between seeing his son graduate or his horse potentially win the Triple Crown and he chose to go to his boy's graduation in the West. The horse was not done and he won the 72nd Travers Stakes in mid-August in two minutes 5.08 seconds to complete the quadruple. Arcaro was suspended so Alfred Robertson (1911–1975) was in the saddle for the fourth title. Whirlaway was voted the Horse of the Year in 1941. Whirlaway retired in 1944 and was put out to stud at Calumet Farm. He died on 6 April 1953 in France.

FIRST

INDIAN DERBY

MAHALAXMI RACECOURSE, BOMBAY, MAHARASHTRA, INDIA.
SATURDAY 30 JANUARY 1943.

The Indian Derby is held on the first Sunday of February at the Mahalaxmi Racecourse, which was built in 1883. The course is based on the Caulfield Racecourse in Melbourne. The first winner was a filly called Princess Beautiful, ridden by the Australian Edgar Britt (1913–2017) and trained by M.C. Patel. Princess Beautiful was the daughter of Short Hand and Roibelle.

FIRST

FEMALE JOCKEY
TO RIDE
PROFESSIONALLY IN AMERICA

JUDY JOHNSON, LONE GALLANT, PIMLICO RACECOURSE, 5201
PARK HEIGHTS AVENUE, BALTIMORE, MARYLAND 21215 UNITED
STATES OF AMERICA. TUESDAY 27 APRIL 1943.

The first woman jockey licensed to ride as a professional in the United States was the English-born Judy Johnson in a steeplechase at Pimlico Racecourse. She finished tenth out of a field of 11. Lone Gallant was 30 lengths behind the winner. In 1927, Johnson had applied to the Maryland Jockey Club for a licence to ride but had been refused. Her second application was accepted due to the shortage of jockeys serving in the American armed forces overseas. After a few races, she decided being in the saddle was not for her and she reverted to her previous calling, that of trainer.

FIRST

VICTORY FOR VINCENT O'BRIEN

**OVERSWAY, GREENPARK RACECOURSE, GREENPARK, DOCK ROAD,
LIMERICK V94 Y17X IRELAND. THURSDAY 20 MAY 1943.**

Michael Vincent O'Brien was born on 9 April 1917 at Clashganiff House, near Churchtown, County Cork, the eldest son of his father's second marriage (to his dead wife's first cousin). His brother Phonsie (see 1951) became an accomplished amateur jockey. O'Brien was interested in horses from his childhood. Leaving school at 15, he became apprenticed to the trainer Fred Clarke at Leopardstown, County Dublin. At 16, he returned to his father's farm and took over when his father died unexpectedly in the summer of 1943. That year, he trained his first winner Oversway, ridden by Noel Sleator. In December 1943, O'Brien went to England for the first time. At the Newmarket sales, he bought Drybob, a three-year-old, for 130 guineas. He was asked by breeder Sidney McGregor to train four-year-old Good Days. In 1944, he managed to pull off the Irish autumn double at The Curragh. Good Days won the Cesarewitch and Drybob dead-heated for the Cambridgeshire. O'Brien had a £2 each way bet on the double at 800-1 and won £1,000.

ONLY
GERMAN DERBY WINNER
EATEN BY STUD GROOMS
ALCHIMIST, HARZBURG STUD, BAD HARZBURG, GOSLAR, SAXONY, GERMANY. APRIL 1945.

Alchimist was foaled on 2 March 1930 at the Graditz main stud farm, the son of Herold. Owner Oberlandstallmeister Burchard von Oettingen (1850–1923) was not impressed with Alchimist and tried to swap him but was opposed by trainer Siegfried von Lehndorff. Alchimist repaid the faith by winning the St Leger and came third in the Diana Prize. In 1933, he won the German Derby ridden by Robert Utting and trained by Ernst Grabsch. He then won with ease two major German competitions, the Grand Prix of Berlin and the Grand Prix of Baden. His career ended after an injury when he was three. The Second World War ended his stud career and as the Allies approached Alchimist fled to the stud at Harzburg. On 15 April 1945, the party reached the River Mulde. Unable to proceed and hemmed in by the advancing Soviet troops, the grooms killed and ate Alchimist. In 1998, a memorial to Alchimist was erected at the Altefeld stud farm.

FIRST

THOROUGHBRED FLOWN TO A RACE MEETING

El Lobo, Bay Meadows Racecourse, 2600 South Delaware Street, San Mateo, San Francisco, California CA94403 United States of America. Saturday 7 October 1945.

El Lobo was flown to a handicapped race in Bay Meadows Racecourse, San Francisco, where he won the race. The pilot, Major William Hucke, won a fortune betting on the horse.

ONLY

JOCKEY TO HAVE HIS LEG
SURGICALLY SHORTENED TO
PARTICIPATE IN THE GRAND NATIONAL

Major W.H. Skrine, Aintree Racecourse, Ormskirk Road, Aintree, Liverpool L9 5AS. 3.20pm, Saturday 29 March 1947.

The 101st Grand National saw 57 horses competing – the largest number since 1929 when 55 took part – and all survived the race. The Prime Minister Clement Attlee was encouraging the country back to work and suggested sporting authorities ban midweek events that would distract the public from their work. As a result of his plea, the National was moved permanently to be run on a Saturday. The weather in the winter of 1946–1947 was catastrophically bad and a freeze thawed into floods, causing 67 days of racing to be lost. There was no racing between 22 January and 15 March 1947. The Grand National, with the going heavy, was won by eight-year-old Caughoo, a 100/1 Irish outsider ridden by 35-year-old jockey Eddie Dempsey and trained by Herbert McDowell, the older brother of owner John McDowell. It was Caughoo's first race in Britain although he had won the 1945 and 1946 Ulster Nationals. He never fell during his racing career. The most inspirational – or perhaps oddest – story of the 1947 Grand National is that of amateur jockey Major W.H. Skrine, who was desperate to participate. So desperate in fact that he underwent an operation to shorten the length of one of his legs which had been injured in the Second World War. Major Skrine rode his horse Martin M and fell off but valiantly remounted and came in 12th.

DID YOU KNOW?

The 1947 Grand National took place in a thick mist which meant the views were obscured. Some years after the race, a fight occurred after Daniel McCann, the rider of Lough Conn, the second-placed horse, accused Eddie Dempsey of taking a shortcut through the fog and the two men ended up in a punch-up. McCann claimed Dempsey missed out a circuit in the mist, hiding by the 12th/28th, and sued him.

FIRST
PHOTO FINISH IN BRITAIN

Great Metropolitan Handicap, Epsom Racecourse, Tattenham Corner Road, Epsom, Surrey KT18 5LQ. Tuesday 22 April 1947.

The first photo finish in Britain occurred in the Grand Metropolitan Handicap at Epsom on 22 April 1947 to decide who came in second. The race is for horses aged four or older and began in 1846.

FIRST
EVENING RACE MEETING IN BRITAIN

Hamilton Park Summer Meeting, Hamilton Park Racecourse, Hamilton Park, Bothwell Road, Hamilton, ML3 0DW Scotland. Friday 18 July 1947.

Two years after the war, Hamilton Park Racecourse became the first in Britain to offer racing in the evening. The meet was in advance of a visit the next day by the Royal Family – HM King George VI, HRH Princess Margaret, HRH Princess Elizabeth and her fiancé Lieutenant Philip Mountbatten. A crowd of 18,000 watched 5/4 Culroy, ridden by three-time Derby-winning jockey Billy Nevett, win the first race, which came one day after the birth of Queen Camilla. The next day, 21,000 turned up to see the newly engaged royal couple whose betrothal had been announced on 9 July 1947.

FIRST

TRAINER TO TRAIN FIRST
TWO HORSES IN THE DERBY

RICHARD CARVER, EPSOM RACECOURSE, TATTENHAM CORNER ROAD, EPSOM, SURREY KT18 5LQ. SATURDAY 5 JUNE 1948.

In 1948, Richard Carver became the first trainer to saddle the winner and runner-up in the Derby. The winner was My Love, ridden by Rae Johnstone and owned by HH Aga Khan III and the runner-up was Royal Drake ridden by Jacko Doyasbere and owned by Léon Volterra. It was the 64-year-old Carver's first visit to Epsom. Even more oddly, the first three horses (Noor was third) were all owned by a combination of the same people. Richard Carver's feat was not repeated until 2002 when Aidan O'Brien trained High Chaparral and Hawk Wing, who came second.

ONLY

JOCKEY TO WIN
US TRIPLE CROWN TWICE

Eddie Arcaro, Whirlaway, Kentucky Derby, Churchill Downs Racecourse, 700 Central Avenue, Louisville, Kentucky 40208 United States of America. Saturday 3 May 1941; Whirlaway, Preakness Stakes, Pimlico Racecourse, 5201 Park Heights Avenue, Baltimore, Maryland 21215 United States of America. Saturday 31 May 1941; Whirlaway, Belmont Stakes, Belmont Park Racecourse, 2150 Hempstead Turnpike, Elmont, New York 11003 United States of America. Saturday 7 June 1941; Citation, Kentucky Derby, Churchill Downs Racecourse, 700 Central Avenue, Louisville, Kentucky 40208 United States of America. Saturday 1 May 1948; Citation, Preakness Stakes, Pimlico Racecourse, 5201 Park Heights Avenue, Baltimore, Maryland 21215 United States of America. Saturday 15 May 1948; Citation, Belmont Stakes, Belmont Park Racecourse, 2150 Hempstead Turnpike, Elmont, New York 11003 United States of America. Saturday 12 June 1948.

George Edward Arcaro was born on 19 February 1916 at Cincinnati, Ohio, the son of Italian immigrants. He weighed just 3lb at birth and grew to only 5ft 2in, weighing at most a little over eight stone. His prominent proboscis led to him being nicknamed "Banana Nose". When he was 12, he almost lost the use of his right leg following a sledding accident.

His first race was in May 1931 at Bainbridge, near Cleveland, and he lost, as he did the next 44 over the following nine months. In January 1932 at the Agua Caliente racetrack in Tijuana, Mexico, Arcaro won his first race. He suffered a fall in 1933 at Washington Park Racecourse near Chicago and was in hospital for the next three months with a fractured skull, broken nose and a punctured lung. He was unconscious for the first three days of his stay. He was back in the saddle by 1934 and rode in the Kentucky Derby for the first time in May 1935, riding Nellie Flag – he finished fourth. He won his first Kentucky Derby in 1938 by a length aboard Lawrin and three years later completed his first Triple Crown on Whirlaway (see 1941), nicknamed "the little horse with the steel springs". He probably would have won the Grand Slam had he not been suspended from riding. He spent 1942 suspended for crowding a Mexican jockey at Aqueduct in New York. An apology might have sufficed but when a steward asked what had happened, he shouted, "I was trying to kill the son of a bitch."

The second Triple Crown came six years later aboard Citation. The eighth winner of the American Triple Crown was foaled on 11 April 1945 at the Calumet Farm in Lexington, Kentucky, the son of Bull Lea and Hydroplane. Citation won, by three-quarters of a length, his first outing as a two-year-old, at the Havre de Grace racetrack on 22 April 1947, a four-and-a-half-furlong sprint, in 54.2 seconds. Just over a year later, he won the Kentucky Derby by three and a half lengths from Coaltown. He won the Preakness Stakes by five and a half lengths – the first time the race had been televised.

On 12 June 1948, Arcaro won his second Triple Crown and Citation became the eighth Triple Crown winner by triumphing in the Belmont Stakes by eight lengths. In 1951, he became **the first horse to win $1 million**. He was then put out to stud. He died on 8 August 1970, aged 25. Eddie Arcaro went on to win the Kentucky Derby five times in his career and won 17 Triple Crown races. On 6 June 1959, he almost drowned during the Belmont Stakes when he was thrown by Black Hills at the final turn and landed face down in a six-inch puddle. A Pinkerton track guard was first on the scene and wisely did no more than lift Arcaro's nose out of harm's way. The jockey had concussion, a neck sprain and multiple contusions of the chest. His last race was on 18 November 1961 when he finished third on Endymion in the Pimlico Futurity. Severe bursitis in his arm forced his retirement in 1962 after winning 4,779 races out of 24,921 starts. He became a TV commentator and then PR for the Golden Nugget Casino in Las Vegas before retiring to Miami, Florida, where he died on 14 November 1997 of liver cancer.

FIRST

WIN BY LESTER PIGGOTT

The Chase, Haydock Park Racecourse, Newton-le-Willows, Merseyside WA12 0HQ. Wednesday 18 August 1948.

Born on 5 November 1935 at Wantage, Berkshire, the son of Keith Piggott, a successful National Hunt jockey and trainer, young Lester started his racing career when he was ten years old. On 7 April 1948, he became an apprentice and won his first race, aged 12, four months later on The Chase, at Haydock Park. He weighed less than five stone and stood just 4ft 6in tall.

DID YOU KNOW?

Apart from his father Keith, a successful National Hunt jockey and trainer, Lester Piggott grew up immersed in horse riding. His mother, Iris Rickaby, won the Newmarket Town Plate on two occasions; his uncle Fred Rickaby won three Classics; his grandfather Ernest Piggott won the Grand National on three occasions – 1912, 1918 and 1919; his great-grandfather Tom Cannon triumphed in the Derby, the 1000 Guineas, the 2000 Guineas and the St Leger; his great-uncle Morney Cannon won the Triple Crown on Flying Fox in 1899, St Leger in 1894 and 1899 and was Champion Jockey six times in the 1890s; his other great-uncle Kempton Cannon won the St Leger in 1901 and the Derby in 1904, and his great-great-grandfather John Barham Day rode 16 Classic winners and trained another seven.

FIRST

RACE BY BILL SHOEMAKER

Waxahachie, Golden Gate Fields Racecourse, 1100 Eastshore Highway, Berkeley, California 94710 United States of America. Saturday 19 March 1949.

Born on 19 August 1931 at Fabens, Texas, William Lee Shoemaker "The Shoe" weighed just 2½lb at birth and in his prime was 6st 9lb. He spent his time at racecourses in California and became an apprentice to trainer George Reeves. Shoemaker rode his first horse in a race on 19 March 1949, at Golden Gate Fields. He finished fifth. On 20 April 1949, Shoemaker rode his first winner Shafter V in a $2,000 claiming race, also at Golden Gate Fields Racecourse. The win was the first of the eventual

8,833 career victories for this 4ft 11in jockey. He had 11 victories in Triple Crown races. He was also **the first jockey to win more than $100 million**.

KENTUCKY DERBY BROADCAST LIVE ON TELEVISION

CHURCHILL DOWNS, 700 CENTRAL AVENUE, LOUISVILLE, KENTUCKY 40208, UNITED STATES OF AMERICA. SATURDAY 7 MAY 1949.

The Kentucky Derby was first broadcast live on television produced by WAVE-TV, the NBC affiliate in Louisville. Shown as it happened in Louisville, a newsreel was sent for broadcast nationally on NBC.

FIRST

PHOTO FINISH IN THE DERBY

EPSOM RACECOURSE, TATTENHAM CORNER ROAD, EPSOM, SURREY KT18 5LQ. SATURDAY 4 JUNE 1949.

The first photo finish at a British racecourse happened at Epsom (see 1947) and then the technology was used at the 1948 London Olympics. It was also used in 1949 to determine the outcome of a Classic race in the Two and then on 27 April 1949 for the 1000 Guineas at Newmarket. The photo finish technology became available on all British racecourses in 1983 and **the first colour photo finish** was used for the Dewhurst Stakes at Newmarket in 1989. In the 1949 Derby, Nimbus (b. 1946) was ridden by Charlie Elliott in a field of 32 runners and riders. Around half a million people turned up to watch the race including HM Queen Mary, HM Queen Elizabeth, HRH Princess Elizabeth and Winston Churchill, the Leader of the Opposition. Nimbus led almost from the start but was challenged by Swallow Tail and Amour Drake and it was these three that were featured in the Derby's first photo finish with Nimbus beating Amour Drake by a head with Swallow Tail another head behind in third. Nimbus was hurt and retired not long after. In 1963, he was sold to a Japanese buyer, was exported and died there in 1972.

━━━•◆•••◆•━━━

FIRST

JOCKEY TO RIDE 4,000 WINNERS

Sir Gordon Richards, Lubbock Sprint Stakes, Sandown Park Racecourse, Portsmouth Road, Esher, Surrey KT10 9AJ. Thursday 4 May 1950.

In 1943, on Scotch Mist at Windsor, Sir Gordon broke Fred Archer's career total of 2,748 winners. Seven years later, on 4 May 1950, Richards rode his 4,000th winner. It was at Sandown Park in the last race of the day when he mounted Abernant and rode him to victory. Abernant (1946–1970), bred by Lady Macdonald-Buchanan, was one of the fastest horses of the 20th century. He was the son of Owen Tudor and Rustom Mahal. From May 1948 until 1950, he won 14 of his 17 races. In his career, Gordon Richards won 4,870 races (from 21,843 mounts), which was a world record until broken by the American Johnny Longden on 3 September 1956.

━━━•◆•••◆•━━━

LAST

MARE TO WIN GRAND NATIONAL

Nickel Coin, Aintree Racecourse, Ormskirk Road, Aintree, Liverpool L9 5AS. 3.16pm, Saturday 7 April 1951.

A quarter of a million people turned up at Aintree to watch the big race. The 1951 Grand National got off to a bad start. Leslie Firth, the starter, let the competition begin with half the runners and riders not ready. He should have declared a false start and called the field back but he did not do that and let the race go on. Jockeys who had been left behind tried to make up ground causing chaos, and a dozen mounts – a third of the field – did not get past the first fence. More horses fell out of the race leaving the 40/1 Nickel Coin, ridden by ex-prisoner-of-war Johnnie Bullock and trained by Jack O'Donoghue, and Royal Tan, trained by Vincent O'Brien (1917–2009) and ridden by his brother Phonsie (1929–2016), in contention. Nickel Coin had it in her and went on to win by six lengths, becoming the 13th and to date last mare to win the Grand National. Just three horses finished the race. Nickel Coin never raced in another National.

DID YOU KNOW?

When she was foaled, Nickel Coin was so weak she could not stand and the attending vet recommended that she be put down. A housemaid said that she would leave if that happened and took over bottle-feeding duties. Nickel Coin slept on a mattress by the fire in the back kitchen until she was sufficiently strong to stand on her own four feet.

LAST

RACE FOR
CITATION

HOLLYWOOD GOLD CUP, HOLLYWOOD PARK RACETRACK, 1000-1050 SOUTH PRAIRIE AVENUE INGLEWOOD, CALIFORNIA 90301 UNITED STATES OF AMERICA. SATURDAY 14 JULY 1951.

Citation, the winner of the Triple Crown (see 1948), won 16 races in a row. His last race came in the Hollywood Gold Cup in the summer of 1951. He won, beating his stablemate Bewitch.

FIRST

KING GEORGE VI AND
QUEEN ELIZABETH STAKES

Ascot Racecourse, High Street, Ascot, Berkshire SL5 7JX.
Saturday 21 July 1951.

The King George VI and Queen Elizabeth Stakes is Britain's most significant open-age Flat race and was first run in July 1951 to commemorate the Festival of Britain. Horses run over a course of one and a half miles every July. The King George, as it is commonly known, was formed from two races, one named for King George VI (established in 1946, a two-mile contest for three-year-olds in October) and the other for Queen Elizabeth (created in 1948, it was a one-and-a-half-mile race held in July for three-year-olds). Major John Crocker Bulteel, the Clerk of the Course at Ascot, had the idea to combine the events and the first race was called the King George VI and Queen Elizabeth Festival of Britain Stakes. The inaugural race was won by three-year-old Supreme Court (1948–1962) ridden by Charlie Elliott in a time of two minutes 29.4 seconds.

LAST

APPEARANCE AT A RACECOURSE FOR CITATION

ARLINGTON INTERNATIONAL RACECOURSE, 2200 EUCLID AVENUE, ARLINGTON HEIGHTS, ILLINOIS 60005 UNITED STATES OF AMERICA. SATURDAY 28 JULY 1951.

A fortnight after his last race, Citation, the winner of the Triple Crown (see 1948), had a final hurrah, being paraded before the 28,000 crowd at Arlington. Citation was put out to stud and died aged 25 on 8 August 1970. He was buried at Calumet Farm in Lexington, Kentucky.

FIRST

KENTUCKY DERBY BROADCAST
NATIONALLY LIVE ON TELEVISION

CHURCHILL DOWNS, 700 CENTRAL AVENUE, LOUISVILLE, KENTUCKY
40208, UNITED STATES OF AMERICA. SATURDAY, 3 MAY 1952.

The most-watched and most-attended horse race in the United
States was broadcast nationally for the first time by CBS affiliate
WHAS-TV.

ONLY

FLAT RACE JOCKEY TO BE KNIGHTED

GORDON RICHARDS, BUCKINGHAM PALACE, SPUR ROAD,
LONDON SW1A 1AA. MONDAY 1 JUNE 1953.

Gordon Richards was knighted in the Coronation Honours, announced
on 1 June 1953 – the only Flat race jockey to be so recognised. The
gong was as much for "his exemplary integrity as of his professional
achievement". On 6 June 1953 – four days after the Coronation – Richards
won the Derby, riding Sir Victor Sassoon's Pinza, at his 28th and final
attempt, winning by four lengths in two minutes 35.6 seconds. There
were 27 runners including The Queen's colt Aureole and Pinza, bred by
Fred Darling and trained by Norman Bertie at Newmarket.

FIRST

DERBY WIN BY LESTER PIGGOTT

Lester Piggott, Never Say Die, Epsom Racecourse, Tattenham Corner
Road, Epsom, Surrey KT18 5LQ. Wednesday 2 June 1954.

In 1954, aged 18, Lester Piggott won the Derby for the first time (of nine), riding Never Say Die (1951–1975), the first American-bred colt to win the race in 73 years, since Iroquois in 1881. A 33/1 outsider, Never Say Die took the lead early on and won by two lengths from Arabian Night and Darius. The joint favourites at 5/1 were Rowston Manor and the French colt Ferriol, both of whom were unplaced. Landau, The Queen's horse, held a prominent position when the field of 22 turned for home at Tattenham Corner, but he faded in the run home. It was a chilly, dull day and the crowd was the smallest since the war. Piggott rode Never Say Die in the King Edward VII Stakes at Ascot Racecourse. Never Say Die came in fourth but the Jockey Club did not appreciate the way Piggott rode and he was banned for six months.

——•◦•×•◦•——

LAST

RACE BY SIR GORDON RICHARDS

Abergeldie, Sandown Park Racecourse, Portsmouth Road, Esher, Surrey KT10 9AJ. Saturday 10 July 1954.

Sir Gordon Richards was at Sandown Park when he was thrown by The Queen's horse Abergeldie. The fall caused the 50-year-old to break his pelvis and four ribs. He was in the Rowley-Bristow Hospital in Surrey until 30 July 1954. Sir Gordon retired as a jockey and became a trainer of racehorses (1955–1970) and a racing manager. Richards died of a heart attack at his home, Duff House, Kintbury, Berkshire, on 10 November 1986. He left £835,624 (£3,150,000 at 2023 values). Of him, Lester Piggott said, "Sir Gordon was the best of his era. He had the strongest will to win and the best balance of any jockey in my time." Lord Oaksey, the chairman of the Injured Jockeys Fund, said, "He was the most wonderful character and an example throughout his career, which was in itself unique.

Nowadays it would be remarkable for somebody to ride 200 winners in a season. He used to do it again and again. It was said of him that no one ever lost fewer races which they should have won. He certainly won many races which no one else would have, or at least very few other jockeys would have. He was of course the ideal weight. Gordon never had to waste or worry about his weight. And he had a combination of strength, brain – tactical brain and knowledge – and the most unconquerable will to win. He would often keep on and on riding a horse where other people would have given up, and would pull the race out of the fire. He was a first-rate after-dinner speaker, humorous and had lots of stories. He was extremely convivial and party-minded, but on the other hand not at all a drinker. He loved winter sports – not skiing so much as curling. He used to go to St Moritz every winter, partly to get fit and partly because he loved curling."

FIRST
COMMENTARY BY PETER BROMLEY
PLUMPTON RACECOURSE, PLUMPTON, LEWES, EAST SUSSEX BN7 3AL. WEDNESDAY 23 MARCH 1955.

For 40 years Peter Bromley was the voice of BBC racing. Educated at Sandhurst, he joined the 14th/20th King's Hussars and after leaving the Army became an amateur jockey until he fractured his skull when a horse he was riding collided with a lorry. His first commentary came at Plumpton on 23 March 1955 and he delivered the line "Atom Bomb has fallen". He commentated briefly for ITV before joining the BBC in 1958. Bromley's first wireless commentary was at Newmarket on 13 May 1959. Six months later, on 1 December 1959, he became **the BBC's first racing correspondent** – the first time the corporation had appointed a specialist correspondent for any sport. Bromley was given strict instructions for the job. He was banned from all commercial deals, forbidden to advertise anything and opening fetes was frowned upon. From 1961 until the summer of 2001, Bromley commentated on the wireless on almost every major race in Britain.

FIRST
FEMALE TRAINER TO WIN
AN ENGLISH CLASSIC

Helen Johnson Houghton, Gilles de Retz, 2000 Guineas, Rowley
Mile Racecourse, Cambridge Road, Newmarket, Suffolk CB8 0TF.
Wednesday 2 May 1956.

In 1952, Gordon Johnson Houghton, the owner of the Woodway stable, was killed in a hunting accident and his widow, Helen (the twin sister of the National Hunt trainer Fulke Walwyn), took over. However, the Jockey Club did not allow women to be trainers at that time so Mrs Johnson Houghton had to employ subterfuge and register the training licences in the names of her staff. Gilles de Retz was foaled in 1953, the son of Royal Charger and Ma Soeur Anne. In 1956 in a field of 19 runners, he was rated at 50/1 for the 2000 Guineas. Watched by a large crowd including HM Queen Elizabeth II, Gilles de Retz put in an excellent race. Ridden by Frank Barlow and "trained" by Charles Jerdein (who later became an art dealer in New York), he won by a length from Chantelsey (10/1), having taken the lead with two furlongs to go.

Asked in 2010 how she felt about the lack of public recognition, she said, "Bloody maddening. It seems so ridiculous in this day and age, doesn't it? Beyond belief. But that's all in the past, and I no longer agonise over it." Gilles de Retz was exported to Japan where he died in 1969, three years after the Jockey Club began issuing training licences to women after it had been taken to court by Florence Nagle.

According to the official records, Jackie Brutton was **the first woman to train a winner over the jumps** when her Snowdra Queen won at the Cheltenham Festival on 16 March 1966 and Norah Wilmot (1889–1980) was **the first woman to train a winner under Jockey Club rules** when her filly Pat won at Brighton on 3 August 1966. Mrs Johnson Houghton was elected to the Jockey Club in December 1977 and died, aged 102, on 4 December 2012.

LAST
RACE BY DEVON LOCH

**Mildmay Memorial Chase, Sandown Park Racecourse, Portsmouth
Road, Esher, Surrey KT10 9AJ. Saturday 19 January 1957.**

The horse that did not win the 1956 Grand National ran his last race in
early 1957. He finished fourth. Devon Loch was put to sleep in 1963.

FIRST
SCOTTISH GRAND NATIONAL WINNER

FIRST
TELEVISED GRAND NATIONAL

FIRST
TELEVISED GRAND NATIONAL
COMMENTARY BY PETER O'SULLEVAN

**AINTREE RACECOURSE, ORMSKIRK ROAD, AINTREE, LIVERPOOL
L9 5AS. 3.17PM, SATURDAY 26 MARCH 1960.**

The 114th Grand National was the first televised, appearing on BBC TV
and presented by Cliff Michelmore after the initial host David Coleman
dropped out with appendicitis. The BBC had 16 cameras dotted around
the course. The commentary team was Peter O'Sullevan (who had covered
the National on the wireless since 1947) commentating on the first of
his 38 televised Grand Nationals, and Peter Bromley, who remembered,
"[The BBC] had built an enormous tower in the middle of the course
so that we could see the majority of the action. It was so huge that
the thing was swaying and I felt most unsafe. Conversely the view was
excellent and having told a few chums of my position for the Foxhunters'
Chase two days before the National, I found the late Ryan Price's wife

Dorothy and Fred Winter's wife Di as guests for the big race. Fred was riding Dandy Scot for Ryan and the ladies thought they would take advantage of the unique viewing position. I applauded them for even managing to climb the endless and precarious ladders up the side of the scaffolding. A further surprise almost made me drop my binoculars when Fred, who had fallen at the Canal Turn, joined us in the crows' nest and the first I knew of his presence was when he tapped me on the shoulder while I was commentating and said 'Watcha cock!'" O'Sullevan was equally nervous, concerned by a restricted view and a monitor that did not function properly.

Eight horses completed the National which was won by nine-year-old Scottish horse Merryman II ridden by 22-year-old Gerry Scott, who had rapidly recovered from breaking his collarbone a fortnight before the race. Merryman II, with odds of 13/2, was the first favourite to win for 33 years. Eighteen horses did not finish the race, of which 11 fell.

<hr/>

LAST

MEET AT BUCKFASTLEIGH RACECOURSE

BUCKFASTLEIGH RACECOURSE, 2 DEAN COURT, LOWER DEAN, BUCKFASTLEIGH, DEVON TQ11 0LT. SATURDAY 27 AUGUST 1960.

Racing began on Wallaford Down in Buckfastleigh, Devon in the mid-1800s but was not overly popular because it was difficult to reach. A new course, Buckfastleigh Racecourse at Dean Court Farm, was opened on 21 June 1883 and racing was held there for more than 75 years. The course was around two miles from Buckfastleigh railway station and a tradition built up for a Whit Monday meet. The races occurred from 1921 until 1939 when the last meet before the Second World War was held on 26 August 1939.

After the cessation of hostilities, the meets resumed. On Whit Monday 6 June 1949, Princess Margaret attended a meet with 25,000 spectators. Buckfastleigh Racecourse was on land that belonged to the

Eton-educated, thrice-married 4th Baron Churston (1910–1991) and he decided to sell up. The land was sold and the last race "under rules" took place in the summer of 1960. There were five meets arranged for 1961 but they were cancelled and moved to other venues in the county. The Dartmoor three-mile Chase was held at Buckfastleigh. The new owners agreed to host point-to-point meetings but the last was held on 19 March 1977.

───◆◆◆───

LAST
MAN TO RIDE AND TRAIN A DERBY WINNER
HARRY WRAGG, FELSTEAD, EPSOM RACECOURSE, TATTENHAM CORNER ROAD, EPSOM, SURREY KT18 5LQ. WEDNESDAY 6 JUNE 1928; PSIDIUM, EPSOM RACECOURSE, TATTENHAM CORNER ROAD, EPSOM, SURREY KT18 5LQ. WEDNESDAY 31 MAY 1961.

Harry Wragg was born in Sheffield on 10 June 1902, the son of a local amateur boxer. He began his racing career as an apprentice at Bedford Lodge, Newmarket. He rode his first winner in 1919 and in 1921 at Newmarket he won the Ormonde Plate on Will Somers owned by King George V. At the time, the received wisdom to win the Derby was to get in front from the start and stay there. Wragg developed a different method – coming in with a late run, earning him the nickname "The Head Waiter" from the crowds that went racing between the wars. He showed the success of strategy, winning the 1928 Derby on 33/1 outsider Felstead, owned by Sir Hugo Cunliffe-Owen.

On 4 June 1930, he won the Derby again riding the Aga Khan's Blenheim, winning by a length. On 9 September 1931, he won the 158th St Leger aboard Sandwich, a bay colt by Sansovino out of Waffles, owned by the 6th Earl of Rosebery (see 1905). On 3 June 1931, he had come third on the same horse in the Derby. This was Wragg's most successful season – he rode 110 winners and was second to Sir Gordon Richards in the jockey table. In 1938, he won The Oaks on Sir Hugo Cunliffe-Owen's Rockfel.

DID YOU KNOW?

Although not coming from racing stock the Wragg family were heavily involved in the sport. Apart from Harry, his younger brothers were successful jockeys. Sam Wragg (1909–1983) won three Classics including the Derby on Pont l'Eveque, while Arthur Wragg (1912–1954) was sixth in the jockeys' championship in 1944. Harry Wragg's son Geoff (1930–2017) took on the mantle of the Abington Place stables. He sold it to Sheikh Mohammed bin Khalifa Al Maktoum in 2009. Another son, Peter (1928–2004), became a bloodstock agent and his daughter Susan married the jockey Emmanuel "Manny" Mercer (b. 1928). He was killed instantly on 26 September 1959 when on his way to the start of the Red Deer Stakes at Ascot, he was thrown from Priddy Fair and kicked in the head. He was 30. Priddy Fair was trained by Harry Wragg. Fellow jockey Jimmy Lindley said, "If he hadn't been killed, he would have been one of the greats. I'd put him in the same class as Lester Piggott."

He was Champion Jockey in 1941, winning 71 races out of 295 starts. In 1942, he became Lord Derby's first-choice jockey and on Watling Street again won the Derby which was run at Newmarket. In 1943, he won the St Leger and 2000 Guineas. He won The Oaks in 1946, the last season before he retired. He had ridden 1,762 winners in 11,658 races. In 1947, he became a trainer at Abington Place, Newmarket. His horses won 16 out of 25 races in that first season.

In 1961, he trained Etti Plesch's Psidium to victory in the Derby where the horse was ranked a 66/1 outsider. The race was watched by a crowd of 250,000 including HM Queen Elizabeth II and HM Queen Elizabeth The Queen Mother. As the field approached Tattenham Corner that day, there were ten horses in contention to win and Psidium was not among them. With a furlong to go, Dicta Drake looked to have the race won before Psidium picked up speed and overtook horse after horse, taking the lead with 50 yards to go. He won by a head. Reports stated that the unlikely victory stunned the crowd into silence "and Psidium entered the unsaddling enclosure in a silence that was positively embarrassing". Injured shortly after, Psidium never raced again. In 1975, Wragg won the Cesarewitch with Shantallah, ridden by Brian Taylor. He retired in 1982 and died on 20 October 1985, aged 83.

FIRST
RACE BY ARKLE

LOUGH ENNEL PLATE, MULLINGAR RACECOURSE, MULLINGAR, COUNTY WESTMEATH, REPUBLIC OF IRELAND. SATURDAY 9 DECEMBER 1961.

Himself, as he was known, was foaled on 19 April 1957 at Ballymacoll Stud, County Meath. He was bought by Anne, Duchess of Westminster (1915–2003), who named him after the mountain Arkle in Sutherland, Scotland. He cost her 1,150 guineas at Goff's Bloodstock Sales in Ballsbridge, Dublin. It was at the home, Eaton Hall in Chester, of the Duchess who was known as Nancy, on 17 December 1989, that Prince Charles told his mistress Camilla Parker Bowles that he wanted to live inside her trousers forever in the notorious Camillagate tape. Arkle, a bay gelding, was the son of Archive and Bright Cherry. His first race was on 9 December 1961 at Mullingar, where he ran in the bumper Lough Ennel Plate ridden by the Hon. Mark Hely-Hutchinson. Arkle, at 5/1, came third of 17 in the amateur race, a length and eight lengths behind Lady Flame (4/1 joint favourite) and Kilspindle (9/2).

FIRST
VICTORY BY ARKLE

BECTIVE NOVICE HURDLE, NAVAN RACECOURSE, PROUDSTOWN, NAVAN, COUNTY MEATH C15 A623 REPUBLIC OF IRELAND. SATURDAY 20 JANUARY 1962.

Arkle's first win over jumps came at Navan in the Bective Novice Hurdle over a distance of three miles. His odds were 20/1 and Arkle was ridden by stable lad Liam McLoughlin. Arkle beat 26 other horses to win by one and a half lengths. He won £133 for his owner. His stablemate Kerforo (who would go on to win the Irish Grand National) was even-money favourite but he was beaten into third place by nearly ten lengths.

DID YOU KNOW?

There is a snack bar at Navan Racecourse called The Arkle Pavilion above the weighing room. The balcony gives a view of the horses in the parade ring below and the home straight.

FIRST

THRILLER BY DICK FRANCIS
Dead Cert, *Michael Joseph, London. January 1962.*

Dick Francis was born at Lawrenny, Pembrokeshire, Wales on 31 October 1920 and, after being demobbed from the RAF, he became a full-time jump jockey turning professional in 1948, winning more than 350 races and becoming a champion National Hunt jockey. In 1953, he began riding for Queen Elizabeth (1900–2002). Probably his most famous ride for Her Majesty was the 1956 Grand National when he rode Devon Loch. In 1957, he was summoned to the Hyde Park flat of the Marquess of Abergavenny, The Queen's racing administrator, and was promptly sacked. Leaving, Francis later said, "I nearly flung myself into the Serpentine, I was so depressed."

Francis began writing a racing column for the *Sunday Express* but, at £20 a week, it was a poor return compared to his jockey money. Five years later, he turned his hand to fiction and his first thriller, *Dead Cert*, was published by Michael Joseph in 1962, priced at 15 shillings. On publication day Francis received a cheque for £300. In 2007, it featured on a list of 100 must-read crime novels. In May 1974, it had been released as a film by director Tony Richardson (who co-wrote it with Lord Oaksey) and starred Scott Antony, Geoffrey Bateman, John Bindon and Judi Dench. Queen Elizabeth was an admirer of Francis's books and he made sure a first edition was sent to her. Francis also did not put sex and bad language into his books because Her Majesty did not approve and once complained about the violence.

It has been claimed the Francis wanted a joint byline with his wife, Mary, but business sensibilities meant his name should feature alone. Rumours surfaced and continue that Mrs Francis had a greater involvement in the writing of the books (certainly the research was hers). The Francises spent seven months each year travelling and researching, and five months writing the books. Each book appeared in time for Christmas and was a guaranteed best-seller on both side of the Atlantic. The hardback would shift 100,000 copies while the paperback at least five times that number. Mary Francis developed polio in her late 20s and her husband had several racing injuries so they spent winters in Florida and Grand Cayman in the British West Indies. Mary Francis, who had suffered from Parkinson's disease for nine years, died on 30 September 2000 and their son said the couple worked together "like Siamese twins conjoined at the pencil". Francis himself said, "Mary and I worked as a team … I have often said that I would have been happy to have both our names on the cover. Mary's family always called me Richard due to having another Dick in the family. I am Richard, Mary was Mary, and Dick Francis was the two of us together."

Following Mary Francis's death no new novels appeared, thus apparently solving the mystery of who really wrote them. Then, in 2006, a new Dick Francis appeared, *Under Orders*, which was followed by *Dead Heat* (2007, co-written with younger son Felix), *Silks* (2008, co-written with Felix) and *Even Money* (2009, co-written with Felix) (see 2009). Dick Francis's novels, whoever wrote them, have been published in 35 languages, sold more than 60 million copies and won a number of prizes.

FIRST

WIN BY WILLIE CARSON

PINKER'S POND, CATTERICK BRIDGE RACECOURSE, CATTERICK BRIDGE, RICHMOND, NORTH YORKSHIRE DL10 7PE. THURSDAY 19 JULY 1962.

William Fisher Hunter Carson was born on 16 November 1942 at Stirling, Scotland. He began working as an apprentice at the Tupgill, North Yorkshire stables of Captain Gerald Armstrong. He rode his first winner at Catterick Bridge Racecourse on 19 July 1962, taking first place with Pinker's Pond in a seven-furlong apprentice handicap.

DID YOU KNOW?

On 10 September 1988, Willie Carson became **the only 20th-century jockey to win a Classic on a horse that he bred** – Minster Son in the St Leger.

LAST

MEET AT HURST PARK RACECOURSE

BYFLEET STAKES, HURST PARK RACECOURSE, MOULSEY HURST, WEST MOLESEY, SURREY KT8. 4.30PM, WEDNESDAY 10 OCTOBER 1962.

In 1887, Hampton Racecourse closed after the Jockey Club refused to renew its licence. Two years later, some local businessmen founded the Hurst Park Club Syndicate Limited with a view to buying the Hampton course and developing it. However, the land was too small for Flat racing so they bought some nearby land to ensure the Jockey Club would have no objections to granting a licence for Flat meetings. Hurst Park Racecourse was opened on 19 March 1890 with the two-mile steeplechase Hurst Park Cup which had a prize of £199. Sir Benedict ridden by Mr Dougall won the race. The first Flat race, The Inauguration Plate, took place on 25 March 1891 and W. Wood riding Ready won the £188 prize.

Located 12 miles from London, by 1900 the course was attracting top-class racing. In 1901, Volodyovski, the Derby winner, was defeated by the Duke of Portland's William the Third. Following the death of Emily Davison (see 1913), two suffragettes, Kitty Marion and Clara Elizabeth Giveen, carried out an arson attack on Hurst Park Racecourse. A number of races including the Victoria Cup and the Triumph Hurdle were run at Hurst Park Racecourse.

The race was used by the military from 1916 to 1918 and from 1940 to 1945. After the war, the course hosted the Winston Churchill Stakes in 1946 and it was won by Preciptic, owned by the Maharajah Gaekwar of Baroda. In 1951, the grey horse Colonist II won the Winston Churchill Stakes – owned by Winston Churchill. Hurst Park Racecourse was very popular with the public but its owners realised the land on which the course stood was more valuable than the course and put it up for sale.

The last race held at Hurst Park Racecourse was the Byfleet Stakes and it was won by the 11/8 favourite Anassa. After its closure, Ascot Racecourse bought 20 acres of turf for use in its National Hunt course. Mansfield Town FC bought one of the grandstands to use at a stand at their Field Mill ground.

FIRST
VICTORY IN ENGLAND BY ARKLE

Honeybourne Chase, Cheltenham Racecourse, Evesham Road, Cheltenham, Gloucestershire GL50 4SH. Saturday 17 November 1962.

Arkle travelled to England for the first time towards the end of 1962. On 17 November 1962, he ran for the first time over steeplechase fences at Cheltenham. Arkle was ridden by Pat Taaffe (1930–1992), who would ride him in all his major races.

LAST

MEET AT WOORE RACECOURSE

Woore Racecourse, Woore, Shropshire. Saturday 1 June 1963.

Woore Racecourse was a National Hunt course near the hamlet of Pipe Gate, opened in 1885, two years after the first racing at the venue which took place in August 1883. It was not the most pleasant course to ride – grazing cows often left deposits, and low-hanging branches on occasion ensured an unfortunate meeting between jockey and deposit. There was also a bridge between navigating the last two fences. Woore was most successful between 1919 and 1939. In 1937, King George VI visited the course to watch his horse, Slam, in the Betton Hurdle. Pipe Gate railway station, which opened in 1870, allowed racegoers easy access to the course but passenger services stopped in 1956. The last meeting – although not known at the time – was on the first Saturday of June 1963. There were 3,996 people in attendance. Terry Biddlecombe (see 1966) won the first race that day and Reg Hollinshead the last – the only race not won by the favourite. Dick Francis (see 1962) competed in his first race at Woore in 1946 on a mount called Russian Hero. Future TV commentator Brough Scott rode his first race at Woore on 21 March 1963 aboard a filly called Tamhill.

LAST

MEET AT MANCHESTER RACECOURSE

CASTLE IRWELL, LITTLETON ROAD, LOWER KERSAL,
SALFORD M7. SATURDAY 9 NOVEMBER 1963.

The first recorded important race meeting took place in Manchester at Kersal Moor in 1681. Unlike most venues, Manchester Racecourse was not a single course but sited around the Manchester area. It hosted racing at Castle Irwell, Kersal Moor, New Barns, Weaste and Pendleton. It was never actually in Manchester. Castle Irwell began hosting racing on 26 May 1847 and continued until 1867 when it was closed for "Christian reasons". From 31 December 1867 until 1901 race meets took place at New Barns, Weaste, a 100-acre area in the Trafford Park region of Salford. **The first steeplechase in Manchester occurred at New Barns, Weaste** in May 1872, and the first running of the Lancashire Steeplechase in 1884.

Racing moved back to Castle Irwell and the foundation stone of the luxurious Club Stand for Manchester Racecourse was laid in May 1901. The first race meet (over jumps) was over the Easter weekend of 1902. The first Flat meeting was held in 1902 at Whitsuntide. The Lancashire Oaks was run at Castle Irwell from 1939 until 1963. On 6 September 1941, the St Leger was held at Castle Irwell instead of Doncaster and was won by the 1st Viscount Portal's Sun Castle, ridden by Georges Bridgland (who would go on to win the Derby in 1947 on Pearl Diver). **The first evening race meeting in England** was held on Friday 13 July 1951 (see 1947). The event attracted a large crowd in spite of the cold weather. At the start of the 1960s the club stand had begun to decay and a new one was constructed, the first with private boxes. However, it could not stop the rot and the owners decide to sell up.

The last race, The Goodbye Consolation Plate, was held on 9 November 1963 and was won by Lester Piggott before more than 20,000 spectators. Despite winning the race, Piggott lost the jockeys' championship that year by one – 175 to Scobie Breasley's 176. Piggott called it "a major let-down after I'd put in so much work to win the title. I was disappointed but it was impossible not to give credit to Scobie, who was winning what turned out to be the last of his four championships."

DID YOU KNOW?

The first victory of a horse owned by HM Queen Elizabeth II after her accession to the throne occurred at Castle Irwell in June 1952.

NATIONAL HUNT JOCKEY TO RIDE 100 WINNERS IN CONSECUTIVE SEASONS

TERRY BIDDLECOMBE. 1965; 1966.

Terry Biddlecombe was born at Hartpury, Gloucestershire on 2 February 1941, the son of a successful point-to-point jockey. He rode his first race on Balkan Flower at Wincanton on 23 February 1957 but was unplaced. His first win came on 6 March 1958 aboard Burnella, also at Wincanton. He rode in the Grand National for the first time on 26 March 1960 aboard Aliform but fell at Becher's. In the 1964–1965 season, 5ft 11in Biddlecombe rode 114 winners and 102 the next season, becoming the first National Hunt jockey to ride 100 winners in consecutive seasons. In 1964, aboard The Pouncer at Stratford, Biddlecombe lost his whip and yelled at the other jockeys that he would give them £10 for their whip. When he received no response, he leaned across and stole one from another jockey and encouraged The Pouncer to a victory by a head. Following his efforts in 1965 and 1966, he was Champion Jockey again in 1969 although with 77 winners. He retired on 14 March 1974 having suffered 47 broken bones and with 905 winners under his belt. Biddlecombe's later life was troubled by alcoholism. He died on 5 January 2014, aged 72.

LAST

RACE BY ARKLE

KING GEORGE VI CHASE, KEMPTON PARK RACECOURSE, STAINES ROAD EAST, SUNBURY-ON-THAMES TW16 5AQ: TUESDAY 27 DECEMBER 1966.

In March 1963, Arkle made his debut at the Cheltenham Festival. Over the course of his career, Arkle won three Cheltenham Gold Cups (1964–1966) but was never entered for the Grand National because his owner Nancy Westminster did not want him to run. In 1964, he won the Irish Grand National at Fairyhouse. By 1965, the Duchess's opposition to the Grand National was wavering and jockey Pat Taaffe (1930–1992) revealed that he would discuss the possibility of Himself running in the 1966 Grand National after the 1965 race. However, four horses died in that race and she decided against entering Arkle. "I just couldn't do it. I am much too fond of Arkle for that. If anything like this happened to him, I would never forgive myself," she said.

Four days before the end of 1966, Arkle competed in the King George VI Chase at Kempton Park. The going was firm and as he leapt the open ditch, he hit a hoof on the guard rail and fractured a pedal bone. Arkle came second to Dormant, ridden by Jeff King. Within three hours of the race, Arkle was given an X-ray and the bad news was confirmed. Arkle was put in plaster for four months before he was returned to training. However, he did not recover full fitness and never ran again.

In October 1968, he began to walk stiffly, possibly due to arthritis, and training was abandoned. On 31 May 1970, aged 13, he was euthanised in his box at Bryanstown House, Maynooth, County Kildare, the home of his owner. He was buried in a field there. The Duchess of Westminster said, "Over the last few weeks, Arkle had progressive arthritic lesions developing in both hind feet. As these became worse, he was in a certain amount of pain. All known drugs and antibiotics were used. In spite of this, no improvement was achieved. In the opinion of my veterinary advisers, his condition was incurable and rather than have him suffer, I had him put to sleep this afternoon." In 1976, Arkle's remains were dug up and his skeleton put on display at the Irish National Stud. Many disliked the decision, including his jockey Pat Taaffe, who said, "I hated seeing his frame up there. I couldn't look at him for long."

FIRST

DERBY WITH AN ELECTRONIC STARTING GATE

Epsom Racecourse, Tattenham Corner Road, Epsom, Surrey
KT18 5LQ. 4.29pm, Wednesday 7 June 1967.

The summer of love was not only notable for music and sex but it saw sporting innovations. The Derby was run in the presence of HM Queen Elizabeth II and HM Queen Elizabeth The Queen Mother and was the first with an electronic starting gate. The front of the stall was held shut by an electromagnetic lock, pressing against spring-loaded hinges. When the starter (in this case Alec Marsh) was satisfied, he pressed a button which cut the current to the locks, allowing all the doors to spring open simultaneously, and the race began. The 1967 race was won by 7/4 favourite Royal Palace (1964–1991) who was ridden by Australian Racing Hall of Fame jockey George Moore who that year came first in the 1,000 Guineas and the 2,000 Guineas as well as the Derby. The outsider El Mighty began at 250/1 but his odds dropped down to 25/1 after the owner of a shop in Peterborough claimed he had witnessed in a dream the horse claiming victory. Oddly, El Mighty went straight into the lead but Royal Palace took the lead two furlongs from the finish and held on to win by two and a half lengths. He was put out to stud after an injury but his offspring did not achieve his own successes. He was put down at the National Stud near Newmarket, Suffolk and buried at the cemetery there.

FIRST

DISQUALIFIED KENTUCKY DERBY WINNER

**DANCER'S IMAGE, CHURCHILL DOWNS RACECOURSE, 700 CENTRAL
AVENUE, LOUISVILLE, KENTUCKY 40208, UNITED STATES OF
AMERICA. SATURDAY 4 MAY 1968.**

The 94th running of the Kentucky Derby was the first hit by a doping scandal. Grey horse Dancer's Image was foaled on 10 April 1965, the son of Native Dancer (the winner of the Preakness Stakes, the Belmont Stakes and voted United States Horse of the Year in 1954) and Noors Image. He was owned by Harvard graduate, amateur boxer and businessman Peter D. Fuller (1923–2012) of Runnymede Farm in North Hampton, New Hampshire. Fuller initially intended to sell the horse in February 1967 but changed his mind and put him under trainer Lou Cavalaris Jr.

Throughout his career, Dancer's Image suffered with sore ankles and so, on 28 April 1968, a vet administered a dose of phenylbutazone, an illegal nonsteroidal anti-inflammatory drug (NSAID) in the belief that it would be out of the horse's system by the day of the Derby. Dancer's Image won the race after a poor start beginning in last position. As the race progressed, Dancer's Image moved up the field and overtook the favourite Forward Pass with an eighth of a mile to go to win. However, the horse failed a post-race drugs test and Forward Pass was declared the winner on 7 May and Dancer's Image put in last place. Ironically, in 1974, the rules were changed and phenylbutazone was no longer a banned substance. In 1986, 13 of the 16 runners were on the drug.

Dancer's Image competed in the Preakness Stakes on 18 May 1968 and finished third, six and a quarter lengths behind Forward Pass. He was again disqualified, on this occasion for bumping the horse Martins Jig. Dancer's Image was relegated to eighth place. Dancer's Image was retired after the race, his ankles still giving him problems. Peter D. Fuller instigated legal action to get his horse reinstated. Meanwhile, the Kentucky State Racing Commission awarded the prize money to Forward Pass.

In December 1970, a Kentucky Court awarded the first-place prize to Dancer's Image but that decision was overturned on appeal in April 1972 by the Kentucky Court of Appeals. Fuller was convinced his horse was nobbled because of his support for the civil rights movement. Put out to stud, Dancer's Image was sent to Glade Valley Farms in Frederick, Maryland and then Ireland and Deauville, France before ending up in Japan, where he died, aged 27, on Boxing Day 1992.

FIRST
FEMALE JOCKEY TO RIDE IN A PARI-MUTUEL RACE IN AMERICA

DIANE CRUMP, HIALEAH PARK RACE TRACK, 2200 EAST 4TH AVENUE, HIALEAH, FLORIDA 33013, UNITED STATES OF AMERICA. FRIDAY 7 FEBRUARY 1969.

Diane Crump was born at Milford, Connecticut on 18 May 1948. She began riding in 1961 and scrimped and saved to buy her first pony. In 1967, Kathryn Kusner, a member of the American Olympic equestrian team, applied for a jockey licence but was turned down because of her gender. She sued the Maryland Racing Commission for sex discrimination and won her case on 30 October 1968. However, before she could compete, she broke her leg in a horse show at Madison Square Garden. Watching the case inspired Diane Crump, who applied for her licence and on 7 February 1969, she became the first female jockey in a pari-mutuel race. She rode the three-year-old 48/1 outsider Bridle 'n Bit at Hialeah Park Race Track, finishing tenth out of 12 runners. Racegoers did not appreciate the idea of a female jockey and she required a police escort to reach the track. Crump recalled, "The crowd was just swarming all over me. They were crazy, up in arms … The hecklers were yelling, 'Go back to the kitchen and cook dinner.' That was the mentality at the time. They thought I was going to be the downfall of the whole sport, which is such a medieval thought. I was like, 'Come on people, this is the 1960s!'" Crump was understandably nervous in the run-up to the race. She went to the paddock still wearing her gold watch. Craig Perret, the jockey next to her in the gate, had to remind Crump to pull down her goggles. A few days later, Crump rode a winner at Florida Downs but the horse was disqualified because he had not been eligible for the race. Crump became the first woman to ride in the Kentucky Derby (see 1970) but was asked by one of the owners of Churchill Downs, W.L. Lyons Brown, not to compete because it would cause too much upset at the track.

FIRST
FEMALE JOCKEY TO WIN A
PROFESSIONAL RACE
IN AMERICA

Barbara Jo Rubin, Cohesion, Charles Town Races, 750 Hollywood Drive, Charles Town, West Virginia 25414, United States of America. Saturday 22 February 1969.

Diane Crump became the first woman to ride a horse professionally and a few days later won a race but her mount was disqualified. It fell to 19-year-old Barbara Jo Rubin to take the honour of the first female winner, aboard Cohesion. Rubin had begun riding when she was seven to strengthen her legs after catching polio. She was hired to train horses and made the move onto the saddle. She was due to make her debut at Tropical Park in Florida on 15 January 1969 but the male jockeys objected and threatened to boycott races that day. Some went further and threw rocks and stones at Rubin's dressing-room trailer, smashing a window. Rubin later said, "I always knew that eventually I'd be able to ride. Getting mad didn't help. My attitude was that as long as I persevered, it was going to happen. When people got mad at me or angry, I'd just smile at them. They'd just get a little madder." The men complained that a woman would be too weak to control a horse. "I never thought that was really it," she said. "The sport had been dominated by men for so many years, and everyone looked up to them as super athletes. I think they felt there would be a stigma if a woman rode, that if a woman could ride, how hard could it possibly be?" She went on to win 11 of her next 22 races. Rubin fell a number of times; one left her with a broken pelvis and neck. She was forced to retire after riding for less than a year, ending a short but historic career.

FIRST

RACE BY NIJINSKY

ERNE MAIDEN STAKES, THE CURRAGH, NEWBRIDGE, COUNTY KILDARE,
R56 RR67 REPUBLIC OF IRELAND. JUNE 1969.

Nijinsky was foaled on 21 February 1967, the son of Northern Dancer (b.
1961) and Flaming Page, at E.P. Taylor's Windfields Farm in Oshawa,
Ontario, Canada. Nijinsky was a distinctive horse; he stood 16.3 hands (5ft
7in) tall with a white heart on his forehead and three white socks. Nijinsky
raced four times at The Curragh and won his first race, the six-furlong
Erne Maiden Stakes with odds at 11/4. In 1970, he became the first horse
for 35 years to win the English Triple Crown – no horse has repeated this
feat to date. His Derby win when he was ridden by Lester Piggott came
in the fastest time – two minutes, 34.68 seconds – since 1936. On 27
June 1970, Nijinsky won the Irish Derby at The Curragh ridden by Liam
Ward. The following month he beat the field in the King George VI and
Queen Elizabeth Stakes at Ascot by two lengths. In August, he lost his
body hair on one flank after contracting ringworm. In September, as the
2/7 favourite, he won the St Leger by a length. Then in October, though
expected to win, he came second in the Prix de l'Arc de Triomphe.

FIRST

FEMALE JOCKEY TO RIDE
IN THE KENTUCKY DERBY

**Diane Crump, Churchill Downs Racecourse, 700 Central Avenue,
Louisville, Kentucky 40208, United States of America. Saturday 2
May 1970.**

It took 96 races before a woman rode in the Kentucky Derby. In 1970,
Diane Crump took that honour aboard Fathom and she finished 15th in
a field of 17. The race was won by Robert Lehmann's Dust Commander,

ridden by Mike Manganello, a mount that had unusually run in a claiming race earlier in his career. Dust Commander sired 1975 Preakness winner Master Derby and 1977 Derby runner-up Run Dusty Run. He died in 1991. Crump retired in 1985 but returned to racing in 1992 before finally calling it a day in 1999.

DID YOU KNOW?

The 1970 Kentucky Derby is not only memorable for featuring the first female jockey, it was also immortalised in print by Hunter S. Thompson. He wrote an article published on 4 June 1970 entitled "The Kentucky Derby Is Decadent And Depraved" for *Scanlan's Monthly* – the first piece of gonzo journalism. The article was illustrated using an eyebrow pencil and lipstick by Ralph Steadman.

FIRST
RACE BY MILL REEF

Salisbury Stakes, Salisbury Racecourse, Netherhampton, Salisbury, Wiltshire, SP2 8PN. Tuesday 12 May 1970.

Mill Reef was foaled on 23 February 1968 at the Rokeby Stables, Virginia, the sire of Never Bend out of the mare Milan Mill by Princequillo. The horse was named after the Mill Reef Club on Antigua where the family of owner Paul Mellon (1907–1999) has had property since 1947. In December 1969, Mill Reef was sent to England where he was trained by Ian Balding (b. 1938), the father of TV presenter Clare Balding, at Kingsclere. Geoff Lewis (b. 1935) took the reins for all of Mill Reef's 14 races. The first was in the Salisbury Stakes for two-year-olds over five furlongs at Salisbury. The favourite was Fireside Chat, the previous winner, ridden by Lester Piggott at 2/9 while Mill Reef was 8/1. However, Lewis steered his horse to victory by four lengths. In third place was Doo Call, ridden by Pat Eddery.

FIRST

WOMAN TRAINER
TO WIN GOLD CUP

ROSEMARY LOMAX, ASCOT RACECOURSE, HIGH STREET,
ASCOT, BERKSHIRE SL5 7JX. SATURDAY 20 JUNE 1970.

Precipice Wood, a grey horse by Lauso out of Grecian Garden and ridden by Jimmy Lindley, was the first Gold Cup winner trained by a woman. He won in four minutes 27.35 seconds.

LAST

RACE BY NIJINSKY

**Champion Stakes, Newmarket Racecourse, Newmarket, Suffolk CB8
0XE. Saturday 17 October 1970.**

Nijinsky's last race was after his loss at the Prix de l'Arc de Triomphe. He ran in the Champion Stakes over ten furlongs at Newmarket. Before the race the horse appeared anxious and did not perform well. He lost to the five-year-old English horse Lorenzaccio. His trainer Vincent O'Brien said the horse had "lost his fire" and so Nijinsky was put out to stud at Claiborne Farm near Paris, Kentucky. He fathered 155 winning horses including the only sire of the Derby and Kentucky Derby winner in the same year (1986). He sired three Derby winners – Golden Fleece (1982), Shahrastani (1986) and Lammtarra (1995). The 1986 Kentucky Derby winner was Ferdinand. Jockey Lester Piggott said, "I think Nijinsky probably on his day was the most brilliant horse I've ever ridden." The film *A Horse Called Nijinsky* was narrated by Orson Welles and released in 1970. After a long battle against laminitis, Nijinsky was put down on 15 April 1992 and buried at Claiborne Farm.

FIRST

YEARLING SOLD FOR
100,000 GUINEAS AT A PUBLIC AUCTION IN BRITAIN
PRINCELY REVIEW. 1971.

Princely Review became the first yearling sold for 100,000 guineas at a public auction in Britain when he went under the hammer in 1971. Foaled in Ireland that year, he did not go on to have the most successful career – Princely Review won one race in seven starts.

FIRST

RACE MEETING ON A SATURDAY MORNING
HAMILTON PARK RACECOURSE, HAMILTON PARK, BOTHWELL ROAD, HAMILTON, ML3 0DW SCOTLAND. SATURDAY 8 MAY 1971.

On the day that Arsenal became the second team of the 20th century to complete the League and Cup Double, Hamilton Park became the first racecourse in Britain to stage a morning meeting.

FIRST

FEMALE JOCKEY TO RIDE 100 WINNERS
MARY BACON, CALIFORNIA LASSIE, THISTLEDOWN RACECOURSE, 21501 EMERY ROAD, NORTH RANDALL, OHIO 44128 UNITED STATES OF AMERICA. WEDNESDAY 30 JUNE 1971.

Mary Steedman was born at Chicago, Illinois on 1 January 1948 and raised in Toledo, Ohio. After training in England, she returned to

America and taught riding. She met and married Johnny "Pug" Bacon. In March 1969, Bacon gave birth to a daughter, Suzie, and was back in the saddle a fortnight later.

She won her first race on 5 June 1969 and triumphed 55 times in 396 races that first year. Her 100th victory came almost two years later. Blonde and beautiful, she modelled for *Vogue* and was the face of Revlon's Charlie Girl ad campaign. In June 1973 – a year after her divorce – she appeared topless in *Playboy*.

In June 1974, *Newsweek* ran a story about women in sport and Bacon's was the only face to appear more than once. That year she was listed in the top ten jockeys for New York's Aqueduct Racecourse. Her career came tumbling down in April 1975 when she went to a Ku Klux Klan rally in Walker, Louisiana. She addressed the crowd of 2,700 people. "We are not just a bunch of illiterate Southern n****r-killers," she said. "We are good, white, Christian people working for a white America. When one of your wives or one of your sisters gets raped by a n****r, maybe you'll get smart and join the Klan." The speech was filmed by a local television station and naturally outrage followed. *The Wall Street Journal* called Bacon "the Klansman's Jane Fonda". Bacon doubled down in an interview with *People*. She said, "People will only worry about what I do from the starting gate to the finish line – not about what I do in my personal life. I'm paid to win races." She also said that the Klan – founded by the Democratic Party on Christmas Eve 1865 – was not a racist organisation and nor was she. "All the records I buy are Motown records. Some of my best friends are blacks," she added. "Once I was called the Bunny Jockey because of *Playboy*, now I'll be known as the one in the white sheets."

The cancellation began almost immediately with Revlon dropping her along with other companies. She also found her work as a jockey drying up. In 1974, she competed in 323 races, in 1975 it was 143 and in 1976 it dropped to a paltry 38. In 1977, her ex-husband Pug Bacon was killed in a car crash. To get work, Bacon had to travel to Japan where she won three races in November 1978 at the Oi Racecourse. In May 1979, she was badly hurt in an incident at the starting gate when her horse landed on her at a small track in East St Louis, Illinois. She sued the racecourse and was awarded $3million but never collected a cent after the course went bankrupt. Another accident on 10 June 1982 at Golden Gate Fields in northern California left her comatose for eight days. She was later diagnosed with incurable cervical cancer. She told her second husband that she was going to Texas to find equine work. On 7 June 1991, she booked herself into room 133 of a Motel 6 along Fort Worth's North Freeway. She paid $25.93 for the room. She visited a pawn shop where she used her American Express card to buy a blue-steel, .22-calibre revolver for $59.95. She lifted the pistol to her left temple and pulled the trigger. She was found lying on the floor, a pool of blood around her head, by a maid about 12.10pm. Bacon died, aged 43, at 1.45am the next day in John Peter Smith Hospital in Fort Worth. She had won 286 times in 3,526 races.

DID YOU KNOW?

There is a statue of Mill Reef at the National Stud at Newmarket. On the plinth below it are the following words:

Swift as a bird I flew down many a course.
Princes, Lords, Commoners all sang my praise.
In victory or defeat I played my part.
Remember me, all men who love the Horse.
If hearts and spirits flag in after days;
Though small, I gave my all. I gave my heart.

LAST

RACE BY MILL REEF

CORONATION CUP. EPSOM RACECOURSE, TATTENHAM CORNER ROAD, EPSOM, SURREY KT18 5LQ. 3.15PM THURSDAY 8 JUNE 1972.

The last (and 14th) race by Mill Reef was a victory by a neck in the Coronation Cup, beating Homeric. Then he fell sick with a virus and did not race. Mill Reef recovered but fractured a leg during training in the run-up to the Prix de l'Arc de Triomphe. A six-hour operation saved the horse's life but his racing career was over and he was put out to stud in Newmarket. With a racing record of 14 outings, 12 wins and two second places, Mill Reef earned £309,225. He was put to sleep on 2 February 1986, three weeks before his 18th birthday.

ONLY
DEFEAT OF BRIGADIER GERARD

BENSON & HEDGES GOLD CUP, YORK RACECOURSE, RACECOURSE ROAD, KNAVESMIRE ROAD, YORK, NORTH YORKSHIRE YO23 1EX. TUESDAY 15 AUGUST 1972.

With the going good, Brigadier Gerard was the 1/3 favourite with Rheingold second favourite to win the Benson & Hedges Gold Cup. However, it was the 1972 Derby winner Roberto ridden by the Panamanian jockey Braulio Baeza (b. 1940) who had the race of their lives winning the one mile, two furlongs, 110 yards race in two minutes 7.1 seconds by three lengths. The time of the Vincent O'Brien-trained horse beat the course record as did Brigadier Gerard, who beat the third-placed Gold Rod by 17 lengths.

LAST
RACE BY BRIGADIER GERARD

CHAMPION STAKES, ASCOT RACECOURSE, HIGH STREET, ASCOT, BERKSHIRE SL5 7JX. SATURDAY 14 OCTOBER 1972.

Brigadier Gerard retired in 1972, having won 17 out of 18 races and earned £253,024.70. His last race was the Champion Stakes, a race he had won the previous year. On both occasions, he was ridden by Joe Mercer (1934–2021) and trained by Dick Hern (1921–2002) and won in two minutes 17.9 seconds and two minutes 7.4 seconds respectively. When Brigadier Gerard retired, he had won more races than any other English Classic winner of the 20th century apart from Bayardo (winner of 22 from 25 starts) and his ancestress Pretty Polly (winner of 22 in 24 races). He was put out to stud. Brigadier Gerard died on 29 October 1989 and his remains were buried in the gardens of the Swynford Hotel, Six Mile Bottom, Newmarket.

DID YOU KNOW?

Brigadier Gerard was named for a fictional French Napoleonic Hussar officer created by Sir Arthur Conan Doyle – he appeared in 17 short stories, a play and a novel. In the tales, the retired Brigadier Etienne Gerard living in Paris recounts his adventures as a young man. As with Conan Doyle's Sherlock Holmes stories, Brigadier Gerard first appeared in the *Strand Magazine* between December 1894 and September 1903. Two collections – *The Exploits Of Brigadier Gerard* (February 1896) and *The Adventures Of Gerard* (September 1903) – were published. There have been four films made so far about Brigadier Gerard (the soldier, not the horse).

FIRST
SCOTTISH CHAMPION JOCKEY
Willie Carson. 1972.

Willie Carson was Champion Jockey for the first time in 1972 with 132 wins, breaking a run of eight consecutive wins by Lester Piggott. Carson retained the title in 1973 with 164 wins. He was also Champion Jockey in 1978 (182 wins), 1980 (166 wins) and 1983 (159 wins).

LAST

RACE BY SECRETARIAT

CANADIAN INTERNATIONAL STAKES, WOODBINE
RACETRACK, 555 REXDALE BOULEVARD,
TORONTO, ONTARIO M9W 5L2 CANADA. SUNDAY
28 OCTOBER 1973.

In 1973 Secretariat became the ninth winner of the US Triple Crown. He won all three races in record times. His Kentucky Derby time is still a Churchill Downs track record for one and a quarter miles. He won the Belmont Stakes by 31 lengths. His last race came later that year in Toronto, Ontario, Canada on a cold, windy and wet autumnal day. A crowd of 35,000 turned up to watch Secretariat win the race by six and a half lengths. The bookies saved money that day because many of the gambling slips were kept as souvenirs rather than being cashed. Secretariat won 16 of his 21 career races, with three seconds and a third. His last public appearance was on 6 November 1973 when he was paraded at the Aqueduct Racetrack in New York before a crowd of 32,990. In 1989, he began to suffer from the painful hoof problem laminitis. When the condition did not improve, he was put to sleep on 4 October. Unusually, he was buried whole – traditionally only the head, heart and hooves of a racehorse are interred.

ONLY

HORSE TO WIN
GRAND NATIONAL AND SCOTTISH GRAND NATIONAL
IN THE SAME YEAR

Red Rum, Grand National, Aintree Racecourse, Ormskirk Road, Aintree,
Liverpool L9 5AS. 3.15pm, Saturday 30 March 1974; Scottish Grand
National, Ayr Racecourse, Whitletts Road, Ayr KA8 0JE Scotland.
Saturday 20 April 1974.

Although a number of horses have won the Grand National and Scottish Grand National, only one horse has won both races in the same year. In the 1974 Grand National at Aintree, Red Rum started the race as third favourite at 11/1. Brian Fletcher was in the saddle for the second year running. Giving 1lb to the Cheltenham Gold Cup winner L'Escargot, Red Rum won easily by seven lengths. It was his fifth win from nine starts so far that season.

Although there was talk of entering Red Rum for another race soon after the National, there were dissenting voices. The horse's octogenarian owner Noel Le Mare let Ginger McCain make the decision. BBC horse racing commentator Julian Wilson wrote to McCain urging him not to run Red Rum again. He said that horses cannot return so quickly after the Grand National to run as well in the Scottish version. Tommy Stack disagreed, "Ginger has made no mistakes with the horse so far. I don't think we should tell him what to do now." Jockey Brian Fletcher was not keen for Red Rum to run either. He later said, "I was totally opposed to the decision. Red Alligator attempted the great double in 1968 and at Ayr he was a dead horse who just didn't want to know – in fact he was never the same horse again. I believed that Red Rum had earned a rest. I voiced my objections, but Mr McCain would not be deterred."

And Mr McCain was correct; 11/8 favourite Red Rum's team included a farrier, Bob Marshall, in case the horse had problems with his plates. McCain said, "Sugar Ray Robinson used to take his own hairdresser, so why shouldn't Red Rum take his own blacksmith?" With Brian Fletcher again in the saddle, Red Rum won the four-mile Scottish Grand National in eight minutes and eight seconds, beating Proud Tarquin ridden by John Oaksey by four lengths with Kildagin third and Canharis fourth and 13 other horses over the 26 fences. Lord Oaksey said, "By all rules he should have been a tired horse in need of a holiday. But to Mr Noel Le Mare's Red Rum, the rules do not apply." The crowd went wild with the *Sporting Life* reporting, "It made the Hampden Roar sound like a mere ripple." The owner of Proud Tarquin, Sir John Thompson, said, "It's a privilege to be beaten by a horse like that."

FIRST

CLASSIC WIN BY PAT EDDERY

THE OAKS, EPSOM RACECOURSE, TATTENHAM CORNER ROAD, EPSOM, SURREY KT18 5LQ. SATURDAY 8 JUNE 1974.

The 196th Oaks Stakes was won by the 3/1 favourite Polygamy, by Reform out of Seventh Bride trained by Peter Walwyn, who won by a length in two minutes 39.39 seconds. There were 15 runners and it was Pat Eddery's first Classic win. Patrick James John Eddery was born on 18 March 1952 at Newbridge, County Kildare, under two miles from The Curragh Racecourse. Eddery's first win came on 24 April 1969 on Alvaro at Epsom Downs Racecourse, after going a whole season without a winner. In 1971, he was named Champion Apprentice Jockey. In 1972, he won the Gold Cup. Two years later, the Horserace Writers' Association voted him Jockey of the Year. In 1975, at Ascot Racecourse, he rode Grundy to a win over Bustino for the King George VI and Queen Elizabeth Diamond Stakes. In 1990, he won the inaugural Lester Award for Flat Jockey of the Year, which he again won in 1991 and 1996 (shared with Frankie Dettori).

Eddery retired in 2003. He won 4,632 British Flat races – placing him second only to Sir Gordon Richards. Eddery once said, "That's all part of the game, going to the Folkestones and the smaller tracks, because it's not Royal Ascot every day. You've got to be out there every day working those muscles, riding in every race if you want to be at your best. There may be more money for a Derby than a seller but that doesn't make you try any harder. A winner is a winner."

Eddery died on 10 November 2015, aged 63, at Stoke Mandeville Hospital. The cause of death was a heart attack but he had had a long battle with alcoholism.

FIRST

SPONSORED GRAND NATIONAL

**AINTREE RACECOURSE, ORMSKIRK ROAD, AINTREE,
LIVERPOOL L9 5AS. 3.30PM, SATURDAY 5 APRIL 1975.**

With attendances falling and revenues dropping, the Grand National was sponsored for the first time in 1975 by Rupert Murdoch's *News Of The World*. The newspaper was first published by John Browne Bell (1779–1855) on Sunday 1 October 1843, costing 3d, and was targeted at the newly literate working classes. It soon became a byword for scandal. In 1891, the *News Of The World* was sold to the Carr family and, in May, Sir Emsley Carr was installed in the editor's chair, a seat he was to hold for 50 years until his death on 31 July 1941.

In March 1892, the paper moved to Whitefriars Street, London EC4 and seven years later moved to Bouverie Street, London EC4. It was George Riddell, the legal advisor to the new owners, that really made the newspaper. He was a workaholic. When he married for the first time, he took just an hour off work for the ceremony and no honeymoon. He claimed that he could not afford one and even though he was phenomenally rich, he never tipped anyone. He hired hansom cabs but refused to hand the fare to the driver, placing the exact money on a wheel, forcing the cab driver to climb down to collect it. He increased the size of the paper and installed new printing presses. He often spent Saturday nights bribing printers and distribution staff to ensure the newspaper got into the hands of its readers. By 1912, the circulation was two million and around three million by the early 1920s. The paper sold four million by 1939. By 1950, the *News Of The World* was selling 8,440,000 copies each week. In 1960, Stafford Somerfield was appointed as editor and *Empire News* merged with the *News Of The World*.

In 1968, a battle for ownership of the title began between Australian Rupert Murdoch and Czech-born Labour MP Robert Maxwell. On 20 October 1968, Somerfield wrote a front-page leader saying that he hoped Maxwell's bid would fail; after all, the *News Of The World* was "as British as roast beef and Yorkshire pudding". In January 1969, Maxwell's bid was rejected and Murdoch took over the paper, his first Fleet Street purchase. On 26 February 1970, Somerfield was sacked. In 1981, it introduced its colour supplement *Sunday* and, three years later, its format changed from broadsheet to tabloid. In the summer of 2011, it was closed by Murdoch after its journalists were embroiled in a phone-hacking scandal. Its last edition was on 10 July 2011 and the final editor Colin Myler. The newspaper's sponsorship continued in 1976 and 1977 before it handed the reins to its sister title *The Sun*. The National has been sponsored continuously, mostly, but not exclusively, by companies that produce alcoholic beverages.

ONLY

TRAINER TO TRAIN FOUR DIFFERENT
GRAND NATIONAL WINNERS

Fred Rimell, ESB, Aintree Racecourse, Ormskirk Road, Aintree, Liverpool L9 5AS. 3.23pm, Saturday 24 March 1956; Nicolaus Silver, Aintree Racecourse, Ormskirk Road, Aintree, Liverpool L9 5AS. 3.17pm, Saturday 25 March 1961; Gay Trip, Aintree Racecourse, Ormskirk Road, Aintree, Liverpool L9 5AS. 3.20pm, Saturday 4 April 1970; Rag Trade, Aintree Racecourse, Ormskirk Road, Aintree, Liverpool L9 5AS. Saturday 3 April 1976.

Thomas Frederic Rimell was born on 24 June 1913 (one year exactly after cricket commentator Brian Johnston) and was a champion National Hunt jockey and horse trainer. He was **the first jumping trainer to earn £1 million in prize money for his owners**.

He won his first Grand National as a trainer in 1956 with ESB, ridden by Dave Dick (1924–2001). The horse came eighth behind Sundew in the 1957 National and sixth in the 1958 Aintree race. He died in 1976.

In 1961, Rimell was back with another winner in the 115th running of the National. Grey Nicolaus Silver was by Nicolaus out of Rays of

Montrose and was foaled in 1952. He was the first grey to win the National in 90 years and another would not triumph until Neptune Collonge in 2012. Nicolaus Silver ridden by Bobby Breasley (1935–2008) took the lead at the second last and held on to beat Merryman II – the 1960 winner – by five lengths. It could have been different though. Nicolaus Silver was targeted by dopers, in the form of a French lady visiting Fred Rimell's stables. Nicolaus Silver took part in the next two Grand Nationals. He came seventh in 1962 and tenth in 1963.

Nine years after Nicolaus Silver's victory, Rimell achieved his hat-trick of Grand National winners. Gay Trip was ridden by 40-year-old Pat Taaffe in his last ride, after Terry Biddlecombe was injured. Gay Trip was the only one of the 28 horses to carry a weight in excess of 11 stone and prior to the National had never won a race longer than two and a half miles. Gay Trip took the lead at the second from last and Taaffe led him to a 20-length win from Vulture in nine minutes and 38 seconds. It was Taaffe's second Grand National victory after winning in 1955 on Quare Times. Taaffe died in 1992, a year after a heart-transplant operation. He was 62.

Fred Rimell's last win at the Grand National came in the middle of the Red Rum triumph era (see 1977). Red Rum had won in 1973 and 1974, come second to L'Escargot in 1975 by 15 lengths and was hoping to complete a hat-trick of wins. Red Rum was ridden by Tommy Stack while John Burke took the reins with Rag Trade. The horse had been ridden by John Francome in 1975 and had come in tenth and last. It was different in 1976 and, despite a battle, he managed to hold off Red Rum to win by two lengths. As Peter O'Sullevan put it, "And it's Rag Trade, gonna win a fourth National for Fred Rimell, John Burke is gonna win the National. It's Rag Trade from Red Rum. Red Rum is fighting back but he can't get to him. Rag Trade is running to the line from Red Rum second and Eyecatcher third, that's how they're gonna finish in the National. Rag Trade is the winner!" Rag Trade missed the 1977 National but competed in the 1978 race. With Jonjo O'Neill on his back, he was the 8/1 favourite but was pulled up after the 21st fence and was found to be so injured he had to be put down. Rimell was also behind two Cheltenham Gold Cup winners: Woodland Venture (1967, Terry Biddlecombe) and Royal Frolic (1976, John Burke). He died on 12 July 1981.

DID YOU KNOW?

It is back to 1956 for the year of Devon Loch and an equine mystery that continues to this day. The Queen Mother at Aintree, with her eldest daughter, had two horses running – M'As Tu Vu making his second appearance in the race with Bert Morrow (1927–2001) in the saddle and ten-year-old Devon Loch, ridden by former Spitfire pilot Dick Francis (see 1962). At 3.24pm the horse was galloping to victory when, with less than 50 yards to go, Devon Loch raised his front legs as if to jump, realised his mistake and flopped onto his belly. Dave Dick, expecting to finish second, took advantage and raced to pass the post first. He said, "Devon Loch had me stone cold. I was a terribly lucky winner." Various theories have been put forward as to what happened to Devon Loch: he had a breathing problem and was starved of oxygen; he was startled by the cheers from the crowd; he tried to jump an invisible fence; he mistook his own shadow for a fence; he saw the Water Jump and tried to jump that; Devon Loch suffered cramp and his muscles temporarily seized up. Vets who examined Devon Loch after the race could find nothing amiss. The mystery continues …

FIRST

WOMAN JOCKEY UNDER NATIONAL HUNT RULES
TO WIN AGAINST PROFESSIONALS

Valerie Greaves, Hexham Racecourse, High Yarridge, Hexham, Northumberland NE46 2JP. Tuesday 4 May 1976.

Valerie Greaves began riding as soon as she left school. Married to a farmer, she became the first lady rider to win against professionals under National Hunt rules, on the David Barron-trained Silver Gal at Hexham.

FIRST

FEMALE JOCKEY TO RIDE
IN GRAND NATIONAL

Charlotte Brew, Aintree Racecourse, Ormskirk
Road, Aintree, Liverpool L9 5AS. 3.24pm,
Saturday 2 April 1977.

The Sex Discrimination Act 1975 allowed women many freedoms. As
a result of the legislation, Charlotte Brew, 21, became the first female
jockey to compete in the Grand National. In the 131st running, she rode
Barony Fort, a horse given to Brew on her 18th birthday. She was not
given much chance of winning. One reporter said, "Barony Fort must
be quite the worst horse ever to be entered." Of the 42 horses that came
under starter's orders, only 11 completed the National and Barony Fort
was not one of them, refusing at the 27th. It was also the year that Red
Rum won his third and final National, having come first in 1973 and
1974, and second in 1975 and 1976. It would be another five years before
any woman actually completed the course (see 1982).

DID YOU KNOW?

For the 1977 Grand National, the BBC wanted to put a microphone
on a jockey so they could have a by-the-minute commentary of what
it was like to ride in the race. The jockey chosen was Tommy Stack,
who was riding Red Rum. However, Stack changed his mind when
he saw the tech he would be required to carry. His replacement was
Graham Thorner, who was riding the 18/1 Prince Rock. The race
began but Thorner forgot he was miked up and as a consequence he
recorded three minutes of swearing, rendering the recording totally
unusable, before he fell at the 12th.

ONLY

HORSE TO WIN
THE GRAND NATIONAL THREE TIMES

RED RUM, AINTREE RACECOURSE, ORMSKIRK ROAD, AINTREE,
LIVERPOOL L9 5AS. 3.15PM, SATURDAY 31 MARCH 1973; AINTREE
RACECOURSE, ORMSKIRK ROAD, AINTREE, LIVERPOOL L9 5AS. 3.15PM,
SATURDAY 30 MARCH 1974; AINTREE RACECOURSE, ORMSKIRK ROAD,
AINTREE, LIVERPOOL L9 5AS. 3.24PM, SATURDAY 2 APRIL 1977.

Red Rum was foaled on 3 May 1965, the son of Quorum (b. 1954) and
Mared (b. 1958) (this is where he got his name from – the last letters of
the names of his dam and sire), and Tim Molony bought the horse as a
yearling for 400 guineas in 1966 for owner Maurice Kingsley. The idea
was to win the two-year-old seller race on the Flat at Liverpool on 7 April
1967. Red Rum dead-heated with Curlicue. Molony had to pay another
300 guineas to buy back Red Rum at the auction which always follows
selling races. Red Rum won twice more before he was sold to Yorkshire
trainer Bobby Renton on behalf of owner Lurline "Muffie" Brotherton.

In the 1972 Scottish Grand National on 15 April, Red Rum finished
fifth. He was bought by trainer Donald "Ginger" McCain (1930–2011) for
owner Noel Le Mare (1887–1980) for 6,000 guineas at Doncaster Sales
in August 1972. However, a day after arriving at McCain's Southport
stables, behind a second-hand car showroom, Red Rum went lame with
pedal osteitis. With no fields, McCain trained his charges on the sand of
Southport beach. Reinvigorated, Red Rum won the first five races under
McCain's tutelage.

In 1973, the seven-year-old was entered for the 127th Grand National
and the bookies made him 9/1 joint favourite with Crisp (1963–1981).
The handicapper gave Crisp 12st and Red Rum just 10st 5lb. The plan
by Crisp's jockey Richard Pitman was to keep him in front but held back;
however, the horse did not see it that way. Pitman recalled, "There's a
long, long run to the first fence, and when he spotted it he couldn't get
there quick enough. Before he touched the ground he could see the next
one. He was almost galloping in mid-air, it was just magic." Crisp was

almost matched by Grey Sombrero, ridden by Bill Shoemark. Pitman said, "The drop at Becher's was 10ft from the top and you had to let the reins slip through your fingers, and sit back in the saddle to act as ballast and keep the horse's backside down, because once his tail comes past your eyeline, you're in trouble. On landing, a lot of horses' noses touch the ground. But Crisp jumped it so cleanly, I never even felt the jolt of the drop."

Crisp arrived at the right-angled Canal Turn ten lengths clear of Grey Sombrero. When Grey Sombrero reached The Chair, he fell and had to be put down. Crisp now led the rest of the field by 25 lengths. As the horse approached Becher's for the second time, he was 33 lengths clear but Red Rum began to put in a kick. As he approached the home stretch, Crisp began to falter. Pitman recalled, "It was like petrol going out of a car. Suddenly his legs started going sideways. He had these floppy ears, which he kept sort of half-cocked, and the strength even went out of his ears. He had gone to the bottom of his barrel. I thought, 'I've got to wake the old boy up, get him out of his reverie.' And I made a mistake that a boy starting out shouldn't make, let alone a senior jockey. I picked the stick up in my right hand to give him a whack, but I had to go right-handed to get round the elbow. The instant I lifted my hand, he fell away left-handed. So I quickly put the stick down, gathered the reins, and pulled him back. But I had to change his stride pattern, and he lost momentum." At the 30th and final fence, Crisp still had a lead of 15 lengths on Red Rum and kept the lead until two strides from the finishing post when Red Rum got his nose ahead to win by three-quarters of a length in nine minutes 1.9 seconds. L'Escargot came in third 25 lengths behind. Crisp ran only once more, at Doncaster the following season, before being retired and joining a hunt at Scotch Corner. He died while out hunting.

For Red Rum, greater success lay ahead. In the 1974 Grand National, Red Rum started third favourite at 11/1. Brian Fletcher was in the saddle for the second year in a row. Giving 1lb to the Cheltenham Gold Cup winner L'Escargot, Red Rum won easily by seven lengths. Only three weeks later, Red Rum won the Scottish Grand National (see 1974).

On 5 April 1975, the 1974 Grand National result was reversed with L'Escargot beating Red Rum, the 7/2 favourite, by 15 lengths. That year saw two horses die at the Grand National – Land Lark suffered a heart attack while jumping the 15th and Beau Bob fell at the second time of jumping Becher's Brook and had to be put down. Red Rum was back at Aintree on 3 April 1976 for his fourth National. Tommy Stack took over from Brian Fletcher in the saddle but he could only equal the result of the previous year – coming second to the Fred Rimell-trained Rag Trade by two lengths.

For the 1977 race, many thought that, a month short of his 12th birthday, Red Rum was too old to compete but the experts did not count on his determination. With the going good to soft, 50,000 people, not discouraged by the rain of the previous two days of the meet, turned up to watch, many of them coming to see Red Rum in his fifth consecutive Grand National. The early betting had Red Rum as joint-second favourite at 10/1 with Andy Pandy and Gay Vulgan, and Davy Lad the favourite at 8/1.

TV presenter David Coleman seemed to suffer some Grand National misfortune when it came to historical events – he missed the first televised National (see 1960) because he was ill and he missed the 1977 event because he was in a contract dispute with the BBC, and Frank Bough took the hot seat in his place on *Grand National Grandstand*.

Forty-two runners and riders lined up for the 3.15pm start that was delayed for nine minutes. Seven horses took no further part after the first fence, five falling, Huperade unseating his jockey John Carden and High Ken being brought down. By halfway, Boom Docker was way ahead of Andy Pandy, Hidden Value, What A Buck, Brown Admiral, Roman Bar, Red Rum, Sir Garnet, Sandwilan, Forest King, Nereo, Happy Ranger, The Pilgarlic, Churchtown Boy, Zeta's Son, Eyecatcher, Collingwood, Carroll Street, The Songwriter, Gay Vulgan, Foresail, and Barony Fort with Charlotte Brew, who was getting a mixed reception from the Aintree crowd. Then Boom Docker inexplicably stopped at the first fence on the second circuit, allowing Andy Pandy to take the lead but he fell at Becher's Brook as did Nereo and Brown Admiral. What A Buck and Red Rum shared the lead. At 3.31pm, another horse got in the way of What A Buck and Red Rum went out in front. Peter O'Sullevan completed his commentary, "He's getting the most tremendous cheer from the crowd. They're willing him home now. The 12-year-old Red Rum, being preceded only by loose horses, being chased by Churchtown Boy, Eyecatcher has moved into third. The Pilgarlic is fourth. They're coming to the elbow, there's a furlong now between Red Rum and his third Grand National triumph! And he's coming up to the line, to win it like a fresh horse in great style. It's hats off and a tremendous reception, you've never heard one like it at Liverpool. Red Rum wins the National."

"I'm glad I've been part of this horse because he's simply tremendous," Tommy Stack told Frank Bough. "I had a good run all the way. The only anxious moment I had was at Becher's second time, when [Andy Pandy] in front of me fell. I went to the side of him and then there was a loose horse coming with me to the Canal Turn. And I had to race him to get to the Canal in case he shut across me to the right. So I just raced him and jumped the Canal marginally in front." Red Rum's eventual winning margin was 25 lengths over Churchtown Boy. Red Rum's win took his career earnings to a steeplechasing record of £114,000. Two horses, Zeta's Son and Winter Rain, had to be put down after falling and a jockey was taken to hospital. The following year, Red Rum geared up for his sixth Grand National but withdrew the day before after going lame with a hairline fracture.

Red Rum retired but, in retirement, he became almost as big a celebrity off the track as he had been on. Red Rum became a limited company and his image adorned tea towels, key rings, fine china and records, and a Red Rum gift shop opened opposite Ginger McCain's stables selling all sorts of memorabilia. Red Rum appeared on TV and opened betting shops, pubs and supermarkets. At least one girl wrote to ask for his autograph. Red Rum died on 18 October 1995, aged 30, and was buried by the winning post at Aintree. Ginger McCain recalled to the BBC, "One of your daft reporter fellows said it must have been like losing the wife when he died. Losing the wife? There are 25 million women in this country."

FIRST
RACE BY SHERGAR
Kris Plate, Newbury Racecourse, Racecourse Road, Newbury, Berkshire RG14 7NZ. Friday 19 September 1980.

Shergar was foaled on 3 March 1978, at Sheshoon – the stud of the Aga Khan IV – near The Curragh Racecourse, County Kildare, Ireland. He was the son of Great Nephew and Sharmeen, described by the National Sporting Library as "one of the most important broodmares of the 20th Century". In 1979, Shergar was sent to England for training. He went to the Newmarket stable of Michael Stoute who the previous year had trained Fair Salinia, the winner of The Oaks, Irish Oaks and Yorkshire Oaks, and Shangamuzo, the Gold Cup victor. Shergar's first race was the one-mile Kris Plate (now The Haynes, Hanson and Clark Conditions Stakes) and he was ridden by Lester Piggott. An 11/8 favourite, Shergar lived up to expectations and won by two and a half lengths in one minute 38.71 seconds.

LAST

RACE BY SHERGAR

ST LEGER, DONCASTER RACECOURSE, LEGER WAY, DONCASTER,
YORKSHIRE DN2 6BB. SATURDAY 12 SEPTEMBER 1981.

Shergar's last race was in the St Leger where he was ridden by Walter Swinburn. On 2 September 1981, the *Sporting Life* ran a story saying that the horse was out of sorts in his training gallops. Shergar's team denied the story and when the day of the race came around it seemed that trainer Michael Stoute had been right as the horse ran well. However, the going was soft which did not appeal to Shergar and when Swinburn tried to gee him to run faster in the home straight, the horse could not be encouraged. Shergar finished fourth, 11½ lengths behind the winner Cut Above. Shergar was retired to the Ballymany Stud, near The Curragh.

FIRST

JOCKEY TO WIN A $1 MILLION THOROUGHBRED HORSE RACE

FIRST

HORSE TO EARN $4 MILLION IN PRIZE MONEY

ONLY

HORSE TO WIN ARLINGTON MILLION INVITATIONAL STAKES TWICE

BILL SHOEMAKER, JOHN HENRY, ARLINGTON
MILLION INVITATIONAL STAKES, ARLINGTON
INTERNATIONAL RACECOURSE, 2200 EUCLID
AVENUE, ARLINGTON HEIGHTS, ILLINOIS 60005
UNITED STATES OF AMERICA. SUNDAY 30
AUGUST 1981.

The Arlington Million Invitational Stakes was founded by Joe Joyce, the father of TV racing pundit Mike Joyce and president of the track, as the first race with a million-dollar purse. The winner gets 60 per cent of the prize money and a trophy. The horses run over a one-and-a-quarter-mile course and it is open to three-year-olds and above. The first race was won by Bill Shoemaker on John Henry (1975–2007) by a nose over The Bart. On 11 December 1983, John Henry ridden by Chris McCarron won the Hollywood Turf Cup Stakes at Hollywood Park Racetrack, 1000–1050 South Prairie Avenue Inglewood, California 90301, thus becoming the first racehorse to earn $4 million in prize money. In 1984, he won the Arlington Million for a second time – the only horse to achieve this feat and also, at nine years old, the oldest. That year he raced for the last time – winning the Ballantine Scotch Classic at the Meadowlands, which was his 39th career victory. In 83 races, he won 39, came second 15 times and finished third nine times. He earned $6,591,860. After suffering a number of health problems, John Henry was put down at 7.05pm on 8 October 2007.

FIRST

JOCKEY CAPTAIN ON A QUESTION OF SPORT

*WILLIE CARSON, **A QUESTION OF SPORT**, BBC ONE, NEW BROADCASTING HOUSE, OXFORD ROAD, MANCHESTER M60 1SJ. 7.30PM, TUESDAY 26 JANUARY 1982.*

The popular sports quiz began on BBC Northwest in December 1968 and was hosted by Stuart Hall before moving nationwide on 5 January 1970 when David Vine took the reins. The first jockey to be a team captain was Willie Carson, from 1982 until 1983. Jockey Frankie Dettori was a team captain from 2002 until 2004.

FIRST

FEMALE JOCKEY TO COMPLETE
THE GRAND NATIONAL

FIRST
GRAND NATIONAL WITH TWO FEMALE JOCKEYS

GERALDINE REES, AINTREE RACECOURSE, ORMSKIRK ROAD, AINTREE,
LIVERPOOL L9 5AS. 3.20PM, SATURDAY 3 APRIL 1982.

Five years after Charlotte Blew became the first woman to ride in the
Grand National (see 1977), Geraldine Rees, 26, managed to complete the
course on Cheers. No fewer than ten horses fell or were brought down
at the first fence in the worst pile-up since 1951; among the casualties
here was Aldaniti, which had won the race in the previous year ridden by
Bob Champion. The race was won by the 7/1 favourite Grittar ridden by
amateur Dick Saunders (1933–2002), who at 48 became, and remains,
the oldest jockey to have won the race. He became **the first member of
the Jockey Club to ride the winner of the National**. Grittar won by 15
lengths, the first clear favourite since Merryman II in 1960. Rees was the
eighth and last finisher (of 39) in the race and it took some effort in the
home stretch as Cheers did not seem to want to finish. Grittar finished
fifth in the 1983 National and tenth the year after. The Grand National
winner died aged 25.

Charlotte Blew also raced in 1982, this time on Martinstown but was
no more successful than she had been in 1977, being thrown off the horse
at the third fence.

ONLY
DERBY WINNER KIDNAPPED BY THE IRA

**SHERGAR, BALLYMANY STUD, NEWBRIDGE, COUNTY KILDARE,
REPUBLIC OF IRELAND. 8.30PM, TUESDAY 8 FEBRUARY 1983.**

In 1981, Derby-winning horse Shergar was retired and put out to stud
in County Kildare. At 8.30pm on 8 February 1983, three armed and
masked men broke into the house of Jim Fitzgerald, the head groom
at Ballymany. His family were locked in a room while he was forced

to show the gang Shergar's stable and put the horse into a horsebox. Shergar was driven away while Mr Fitzgerald was put into a van and driven around for four hours. He was freed near the village of Kilcock, around 20 miles from Ballymany. He was told not to call the police but to await instructions and was given the name King Neptune by which he could identify the gang.

Back at the stud, Mr Fitzgerald contacted the stud manager Ghislain Drion, who tried to call the Aga Khan. He finally made contact at 4am and was told to call the police. The eight-hour delay meant the trail had gone cold. Before Mr Fitzgerald could get back to the stud, a call was made asking for £40,000 (later increased to £52,000) and any negotiations must be made by journalists Derek Thompson and John Oaksey of ITV and Peter Campling from *The Sun*. The three men were told to go to the Europa Hotel, Great Victoria Street, Belfast BT2 7AP. A call was made telling them to go to the home of horse trainer Jeremy Maxwell. The police told Derek Thompson to keep any caller on the line for as long as possible so the call could be traced.

At 1.30am, Mr Thompson managed to keep chatting for 90 seconds, more than long enough for a trace. It was revealed that the tracer had finished their shift at midnight and had gone home. On 9 February, Ghislain Drion received a call asking for £2 million but he had trouble understanding the thick Irish accent and the Irishman had problems with M. Drion's heavily accented French. At 7am on 12 February, another call was made and the caller said that there had been a problem and Shergar was dead.

In 1999, Sean O'Callaghan (1954–2017), a former member of the IRA turned supergrass, said that the horse was stolen to raise funds for the terrorist organisation. He claimed that Shergar was machine-gunned to death four days after the kidnap when he panicked and hurt a leg. No arrests have been made regarding the kidnapping, no trace of Shergar has been found but it is thought his remains were buried near Aughnasheelin, near Ballinamore, County Leitrim. The IRA has never admitted any role in the theft.

FIRST
WOMAN TO TRAIN A
GRAND NATIONAL WINNER

JENNY PITMAN, CORBIERE, AINTREE RACECOURSE, ORMSKIRK ROAD, AINTREE, LIVERPOOL L9 5AS. SATURDAY 9 APRIL 1983.

Ten years after her husband Richard came second in the Grand National to Red Rum, riding Crisp, Jenny Pitman became the first woman to train a National winner. In 1975, she obtained her trainer's licence and that same year Corbiere was foaled, the son of Harwell and Ballycashin, and in December 1982 he won the Welsh Grand National. Five months later, he triumphed in the Grand National, ridden by Ben De Haan and carrying 158 pounds. The bookies gave him odds of 13/1. Corbiere took the lead after the second jumping of Valentine's Brook and won from Greasepaint by three-quarters of a length. He was placed third in the 1984 and 1985 Grand Nationals, fell at the fourth fence in the 1986 race and was 12th in 1987. He retired and died in 1988. Apart from Corbiere, Jenny Pitman also won the 1983 Welsh Grand National with Burrough Hill Lad ridden by John Francome and the 1986 with Stearsby with Graham Bradley on his back. In 1995, she won her second Grand National with Royal Athlete. She has also trained two Cheltenham Gold Cup winners with Burrough Hill Lad in 1984 and Garrison Savanah in 1991. Jenny Pitman retired in 1999.

LAST
DERBY VICTORY FOR LESTER PIGGOTT

TEENOSO, EPSOM RACECOURSE, TATTENHAM CORNER ROAD, EPSOM, SURREY KT18 5LQ. WEDNESDAY 1 JUNE 1983.

In 1982, Lester Piggott did not ride in the Derby for the first time in 20 years because his intended horse, Simply Great, suffered an injury shortly before the race. For a time, it looked as if he would not compete in 1983 either. He was asked if he would be interested in riding Tolomeo, the 2000 Guineas runner-up trained by Luca Cumani, but Piggott felt Tolomeo was not a mile and a half racer so he declined. Geoff Wragg (see 1961) asked Piggott if Eric Moller's Teenoso would appeal.

Teenoso was born on 7 April 1980, the son of Youth and Furioso. He made his racing debut over six furlongs at Newmarket in August 1982 but was unplaced. In his first year of racing, he made £262. Wragg recalled, "Lester came and rode Teenoso in a gallop on [Newmarket's] Racecourse Side on the Saturday before the Derby. Teenoso worked very well and Lester told me that he would gallop Tolomeo on Sunday, then speak to Vincent [O'Brien] and let me know his decision later on Sunday. Despite his reputation Lester is a man of his word. If he said he would let you know on a certain day, he would never let you down. He rang up on Sunday as agreed and told me he would ride Teenoso. From that moment on I was highly confident we would win the Derby." And so it proved, although the weather tried to intervene. Several meetings had been cancelled that spring because of waterlogging and half an inch of rain fell on Epsom in an hour the night before the Derby, leaving the going to be heavy for the first time in more than half a century.

The 1983 Derby was the 204th running of the race. It was Piggott's ninth and last Derby win albeit in the slowest time of the 20th century – two minutes 49.07 seconds. Teenoso won by three lengths. In the autumn of 1999, Teenoso developed thrombosis and was put down on 4 October at Pitts Farm Stud.

FIRST

HORSE TO COST $10 MILLION AND NEVER RACE

SNAAFI DANCER, KEENELAND SELECT SALES, 4201 VERSAILLES ROAD, LEXINGTON, KENTUCKY 40510, UNITED STATES OF AMERICA. TUESDAY 19 JULY 1983.

Snaafi Dancer was foaled on 25 February 1982, the son of Northern Dancer and My Bupers. The horse was highly regarded by its breeders and was put up for auction at the Keeneland Select Sales in 1983. Things looked promising when the bidding opened at $1million and within ten seconds had reached $3million and took just 45 seconds to beat the previous record, reaching $4½million. The bidding ended at $10.2million with Sheikh Mohammed al Maktoum seeing off Robert Sangster for the horse; he dropped out when the price hit $10million. Sangster's trainer Vincent O'Brien said, "He was the best-looking horse in the sale." Asked if any horse was really worth that amount of money, he said, "That'll have to be proved, but it's quite possible he is." O'Brien could not have been more wrong. The seller Crescent Farm owned by coal merchant Donald Johnson offered two horses in the auction. He said, "I knew he was a nice colt and would bring a lot of money, but I never thought it would bring that kind of money. The nice part of it was that they weren't using Monopoly money." Snaafi Dancer was sent to Al Maktoum's Aston Upthorpe Stud at The Stud House, Hagbourne Road,

Didcot, Oxfordshire OX11 9EE. The horse turned out to be a financial disaster – he was so slow in training that to save his blushes he was never run in public. He was put out to stud in the hope of recouping some of the outlay but that was also unsuccessful. In two years, he fathered only four children, none of whom had great success on the track.

FIRST

FEMALE JOCKEY TO WIN
THE IRISH GRAND NATIONAL

Anne Ferris, Bentom Boy, Fairyhouse Racecourse, Fairyhouse Road, Ballybin, Ratoath, County Meath A85 XK30 Republic of Ireland. Monday 23 April 1984.

Amateur jockey Mrs Harry Ferris became the first woman to win the Irish Grand National when she rode 33/1 Bentom Boy to victory. The nine-year-old victor was trained by Willie Rooney, Mrs Ferris's father. She died on 22 June 2022 at Daisy Hill Hospital, 5 Hospital Road, Newry BT35 8DR Northern Ireland, aged 81.

FIRST

FEMALE TRAINER IN BELMONT STAKES

Sarah Lundy, Minstrel Star, Belmont Park Racecourse, 2150 Hempstead Turnpike, Elmont, New York 11003, United States of America. Saturday 9 June 1984.

In 1984, Sarah Lundy became the first female trainer in the Belmont Stakes when she trained Minstrel Star – the horse came in 11th. Sarah A. Lundy was born on 26 August 1954 and, in 690 races, Lundy won 85.

LAST
GRAND NATIONAL FENCE NAMED
AFTER A COMPETITOR
FOINAVON, AINTREE RACECOURSE, ORMSKIRK ROAD, AINTREE, LIVERPOOL L9 5AS. 1984.

Foinavon was not expected to do well in the 1967 Grand National. Indeed, the bookies placed him at 100/1 and that seemed justified when he had just one mention by the BBC commentary team of Peter O'Sullevan, Bob Haynes, Michael O'Hehir and Michael Seth-Smith in the first six or so minutes of the race. Foinavon's owner (Cyril Watkins) and trainer (John Kempton) did not even bother to travel to Aintree to watch the race on 8 April. Then a remarkable thing happened – as the field approached the 23rd fence there was a melee of horses as Popham Down, who had continued running despite unseating his rider at the first, ran towards his right at the 23rd fence, slamming into Rutherfords, unseating Johnny Leech, his jockey. Other horses could not avoid the fence and The Fossa, Norther, Dun Widdy, Rondetto, Harry Black, Princeful, Leedsy, Different Class and Limeking were all knocked out of the race. As Michael O'Hehir put it, "Rutherfords has been hampered, and so has Castle Falls; Rondetto has fallen, Princeful has fallen, Norther has fallen, Kirtle Lad has fallen, The Fossa has fallen, there's a right pile-up … And now, with all this mayhem, Foinavon has gone off on his own! He's about 50, 100 yards in front of everything else!" Foinavon had been in 22nd place at Becher's Brook and this gave his jockey John Buckingham enough time to guide Foinavon out of the way of the scuffle and jump the fence cleanly.

At one stage Foinavon was about 150 yards ahead of the second horse but some of the other jockeys remounted and rejoined the race, giving chase. None of them had the time or speed, however, to catch the blinkered Foinavon and in the end he raced home ahead of Honey End, the 15/2 favourite ridden by Josh Gifford, by 15 lengths in a time of nine minutes 49.4 seconds. John Buckingham said in an interview in

2007, "I had to make an instant decision, so I steered Foinavon to the outside to get away. You've got to give a lot of credit to the horse. He was galloping into a wall of horses, some upside down in the fence. It wasn't until the Canal Turn that I knew I was on my own. From then on I was just concentrating on keeping him going. He was a lazy old bugger, but I knew he wouldn't fall." Foinavon took part in the 1968 National but this time did fall – at the Water Jump.

He died in 1971 following an attack of colic. He was 13. After the race, O'Hehir suggested naming the 4ft 6in high, 3ft wide fence (the smallest on the course) at which all the trouble occurred after the winning horse and in 1984 Aintree officially named the seventh and 23rd fence Foinavon.

＊＊＊

ONLY

JOCKEY TO RIDE THE WINNER OF THE KENTUCKY DERBY AND THE DERBY

Steve Cauthen, Kentucky Derby, Churchill Downs Racecourse, 700 Central Avenue, Louisville, Kentucky 40208 United States of America. Saturday 6 May 1978; Derby, Epsom Racecourse, Tattenham Corner Road, Epsom, Surrey KT18 5LQ. Wednesday 5 June 1985.

Born on 1 May 1960 at Covington, Kentucky, Steve Cauthen made his racing debut at Churchill Downs on 12 May 1976 – riding King of Swat, he came last. It took him under a week to ride his first winner (Red Pipe) at River Downs. In 1978, he became the youngest jockey to win the US Triple Crown, aboard Affirmed – **the last US Triple Crown winner of the 20th century**.

In May, he rode the 9/5 horse in the 104th Kentucky Derby, winning by one and a half lengths over Alydar. The same year, he was named *Sports Illustrated* Sportsman of the Year. Moving to Europe, in April 1979 Cauthen rode Marquee Universal to victory at Salisbury in his inaugural race in the UK. Cauthen was British Champion Jockey three times, and won ten English Classic races including the 2000 Guineas, the Derby twice, and the St Leger three times. Seven years later, on 5 June 1985, with the going good, and 14 horses running, Cauthen rode the 9/4 favourite Slip Anchor trained by Henry Cecil, bred and owned by the 9th Baron Howard de Walden (1912–1999) in the 206th Derby. Cauthen and Slip Anchor took the lead from the start and held on, being ten lengths ahead of the field as he turned into the straight. In two minutes 36.23 seconds, Slip Anchor won by seven lengths from Law Society – the first Derby winner to lead all the way since Coronach in 1926. Cauthen – the first American jockey to win the Derby – said, "This horse kills them before they have a chance to get at him." The race was watched by 250,000 including Queen Elizabeth II.

Slip Anchor was foaled on 5 April 1982, the son of Shirley Heights and Sayonara and grandson of Mill Reef (see 1970). Both Shirley Heights and Mill Reef were both previous Derby winners. As Slip Anchor aged, he became difficult to handle and retired in 1986. Slip Anchor was put down on 22 September 2011 at Plantation Stud at Exning, Suffolk. He was 29.

⬥•✦•⬥

ONLY
JOCKEY "KIDNAPPED" ON EVE OF GRAND NATIONAL
STEVE SMITH-ECCLES, AINTREE RACECOURSE, ORMSKIRK ROAD, AINTREE, LIVERPOOL L9 5AS. FRIDAY 4 APRIL 1986.

On the day before the 1986 Grand National, jockey Steve Smith-Eccles was having a kip in the back of his car when he was shaken awake. The car had been twocked with him inside. He remembered, "The thief was as shocked as I was when he saw me bob up; he panicked and eventually pulled onto the hard shoulder, got out and bolted." The next day, Smith-Eccles rode the 22/1 Classified to third place, 20 lengths behind Young Driver before 75,637 spectators.

FIRST

FEMALE JOCKEY TO WIN RACE AGAINST
PROFESSIONALS AT CHELTENHAM

GEE ARMYTAGE, MILDMAY OF FLETE CHASE, CHELTENHAM
RACECOURSE, EVESHAM ROAD, CHELTENHAM,
GLOUCESTERSHIRE GL50 4SH. WEDNESDAY 18 MARCH 1987.

In 1987, Gee Armytage became the first woman to ride the winner of a Cheltenham Festival race against professional jockeys when she won the Mildmay of Flete Chase on Gee-A. The two miles four furlongs and 127 yard race was named for Old Etonian amateur National Hunt jockey Anthony Mildmay, who rode three winners at the Cheltenham Festival. The first was due to be run in March 1951 but was delayed for a month because of a waterlogged course – somewhat ironically since Mildmay had drowned aged 41 while swimming off Devon on 12 May 1950.

FIRST

BRITISH VICTORY FOR
FRANKIE DETTORI

LIZZIE HARE, GOODWOOD RACECOURSE,
SELHURST PARK ROAD, CHICHESTER PO18 0PS.
TUESDAY 9 JUNE 1987.

Born as Lanfranco Dettori in Milan, Italy on 15 December 1970, Frankie Dettori's father Gianfranco Dettori won the 2000 Guineas on 3 May 1975 and 28 April 1976. Dettori junior left school aged 13 to become a stable boy. On 16 November 1986, he rode Rif to victory at Turin, the first of 16 winners in Italy. His first English victory came on Lizzie Hare at Goodwood in the summer of 1987 and in 1990 he became the first teenager since Lester Piggott to ride 100 winners.

ONLY
DERBY WINNER JAILED FOR TAX EVASION
ONLY
DERBY WINNER TO HAVE
ROYAL HONOUR ANNULLED

Lester Piggott, Ipswich Crown Court, 1 Russell Road, Ipswich, Suffolk
IP1 2AG. Friday 23 October 1987; Cabinet Office, 70 Whitehall, London
SW1A 2AS. Thursday 6 June 1988.

A glittering career ended in disgrace and prison for Lester Piggott when
he was jailed for three years after being found guilty of a tax fraud worth
£3¼million. Piggott, 51, did not react when Mr Justice Farquharson
passed sentence but his wife, Susan, collapsed in tears as he was taken
to Norwich prison. Piggott was accused of failing to report to the Inland
Revenue £1,359,726 from additional riding income and for 14 years
from 1971 he omitted income of £1,031,697 from bloodstock operations.
Piggott used different names to channel his earnings into secret bank
accounts in Switzerland, the Bahamas, Singapore and the Cayman
Islands. The case was the biggest individual income tax fraud case brought
in Britain and the sentence is the stiffest to be passed for a personal tax
fraud. HM Customs and the Inland Revenue teamed up to investigate
Piggott in a case codenamed Centaur after the mythological half-man,
half-horse beast. Piggott's barrister, John Mathew QC, appealed for
a lenient sentence but Mr Justice Farquharson said he could not "pass
over" the enormousness of Piggott's VAT and income tax evasion because
that would be an invitation for others to cheat. With time off for good
behaviour, he served a year and a day in prison. On 6 June 1988, his OBE,
awarded in the 1975 New Year's Honours List, was annulled.

Out of jail after a year and a day and just a dozen days out of his second
retirement, Piggott won the $1million Breeders' Cup Mile in America
on Royal Academy in 1990 and the 2000 Guineas on 2 May 1992 on

Rodrigo de Triano – his 30th British Classic win. Piggott finally retired in 1995. He returned in 2001 to take part in a special race at the Melbourne Cup meeting. In all, he rode 4,493 winners and was named Champion Jockey 11 times between 1960 and 1982. Piggott died on 29 May 2022 at Geneva, Switzerland, aged 86.

DID YOU KNOW?

Apart from being very tight with money, Piggott was also partially deaf. The story is told of a jockey's valet who whispered in his ear: "Lester, can you lend me £5?" Piggott indicated he could not hear, so he whispered in his other ear: "Can you lend me £10?" to which the jockey replied: "Try the £5 ear again."

FIRST
JOCKEY TO RUN IN THE LONDON MARATHON
STUART SHILSTON, LONDON MARATHON, LONDON.
SUNDAY 23 APRIL 1989.

Jockey Stuart Shilston ran in the 1989 London Marathon to raise money for disabled National Hunt jockey Jessica Charles-Jones. She rode for Lambourn trainer Rod Simpson. In August 1986, she married fellow jockey Gareth Charles-Jones (b. 16 March 1961) and made news when they each rode a winner at the same meeting. She had ridden 14 winners before she suffered a fall, aged 23, from 33/1 outsider St Anlo on 3 October 1988 at Southwell. She broke her back, which left her paralysed from the chest down and wheelchair-bound. Not long after, Gareth Charles-Jones was diagnosed with lymphatic cancer and had to have a double hip replacement for bone cancer in his joints. Jessica Charles-Jones died from a heart attack on 8 September 2010, aged 45.

ONLY

JOCKEY TO BECOME A PAGE 3 GIRL

Pamela Rouse, The People, *Holborn Circus, London. EC1P 1DQ. Sunday 25 June 1989.*

Pamela Rouse's father was jockey Brian Rouse and for a time she attempted to follow in his stirrups. However, she decide to take another career path and in the summer of 1989 she appeared almost in silks in a tabloid newspaper. She said, "I have always had a secret ambition to be a Page 3 Girl. I don't think my dad really approves."

ONLY

HORSE TO WIN 2000 GUINEAS, DERBY, ECLIPSE STAKES AND KING GEORGE VI AND QUEEN ELIZABETH STAKES IN SAME YEAR

Nashwan, 2000 Guineas, Newmarket Racecourse, Newmarket, Suffolk CB8 0XE. Saturday 6 May 1989; Derby, Epsom Racecourse, Tattenham Corner Road, Epsom, Surrey KT18 5LQ. Wednesday 7 June 1989; Eclipse Stakes, Sandown Park Racecourse, Portsmouth Road, Esher, Surrey KT10 9AJ. Saturday 8 July 1989; King George VI and Queen Elizabeth Stakes, Ascot Racecourse, High Street, Ascot, Berkshire SL5 7JX. Saturday 22 July 1989.

Nashwan was foaled on 1 March 1986, the son of Blushing Groom and Height of Fashion, at Hamdan Al Maktoum's Shadwell Farm, Lexington, Kentucky. Nashwan was trained by Major Dick Hern and ridden by Willie Carson. His first Classic success in 1989 came at Newmarket when he started the 2000 Guineas as the 3/1 favourite. Nashwan took the lead with a quarter of a mile to go and won by a length. A month and a day later, Nashwan and Willie Carson were at a cold and damp Epsom for the Derby. There were around half a million spectators including HM The Queen. Nashwan began as 5/4 favourite against 11 mounts. Nashwan won by five lengths from the 500/1 outsider Terimon. Nashwan was the first horse to complete the Guineas–Derby double since Nijinsky in 1970.

Another month and a day later, the horse and jockey were at Sandown Park for the Eclipse Stakes when 2/5 favourite Nashwan took the lead coming up to the final furlong and won by five lengths from outsider Opening Verse. Nashwan started the all-ages King George VI and Queen Elizabeth Stakes over one and a half miles at Ascot as the 2/9 favourite. Thanks to Carson's skill, Nashwan won by a neck. Nashwan retired at the end of the year. He died at Shadwell Stud on 19 July 2002 from complications after leg surgery.

DID YOU KNOW?

Bitmap Brothers, a computer game developer, has included references to Nashwan in many of its games.

LAST

VICTORY FOR BILL SHOEMAKER

BEAU GENIUS, HALLANDALE HANDICAP, GULFSTREAM PARK, 901 SOUTH FEDERAL HIGHWAY, HALLANDALE BEACH, FLORIDA 33009, UNITED STATES OF AMERICA. SATURDAY 20 JANUARY 1990.

The last and 8,833rd win in Bill Shoemaker's career came aboard Beau Genius in 1990.

LAST

RACE FOR BILL SHOEMAKER

PATCHY GROUNDFOG, SANTA ANITA PARK, 285 WEST HUNTINGTON DRIVE, ARCADIA, CALIFORNIA 91007 UNITED STATES OF AMERICA. SATURDAY 3 FEBRUARY 1990.

The last and 40,350th race in Bill Shoemaker's career was publicised as "The Legend's Last Ride". He came fourth. After his retirement he became a trainer although his record did not compare to that in the saddle. Among his clients was the composer Burt Bacharach. A year after his retirement from racing, on 8 April 1991, while driving drunk he overturned his Ford Bronco II in San Dimas, California, and was left paralysed from the neck down and confined to a wheelchair for the rest of his life. Despite being almost double the limit for driving in California, he refused to accept blame for the accident and sued Ford for faulty design and the California Department of Transportation for not putting rails along the motorway. Remarkably, despite him being drunk when driving, Ford made a $1 million payment to Shoemaker. He finally retired on 3 November 1997, winning 90 of 714 races. Shoemaker died aged 72 on 12 October 2003.

ONLY
VOID GRAND NATIONAL
AINTREE RACECOURSE, ORMSKIRK ROAD, AINTREE, LIVERPOOL L9 5AS. 3.50PM, SATURDAY 3 APRIL 1993.

The 1993 Grand National – the 147th – was due to be run on the first Saturday in April. The starter Keith Brown, officiating his last National before retirement, told the riders to "take a turn" and walk to the tape. There were 15 animal rights demonstrators down the field who had already caused a delay to the start. He pushed the button to start the race but the tape did not rise properly and indeed some horses became caught up in it. Mr Brown immediately raised a red flag to signify a false start and all the horses were recalled before they reached the first fence. The horses lined up again but once more the starting tape failed to rise properly – it caught around Richard Dunwoody's throat – but the recall official Ken Evans did not notice the second false start and did not wave his flag so 30 of the 39 runners were unaware of the second false start. Of it, BBC commentator Peter O'Sullevan said, "And they're away – oh, and once again the tape has snagged, and it's a recall … It was caught round Richard Dunwoody's neck, the tape. And they've been recalled – but the majority don't realise that it is a recall! They're going down to jump the first, they're going to."

Officials tried to stop the race and the crowd loudly booed. As the horses reached The Chair more stewards waved red flags but the jockeys thought they were the demonstrators and continued. Peter Scudamore on Captain Dibble stopped because he saw Martin Pipe, his trainer, desperately waving at him. It was at the final fence of the first circuit that most jockeys realised something was wrong and pulled up. Fourteen runners and riders continued onto the second circuit. Sure Metal, ridden by Seamus O'Neill, and Howe Street, with Andy Orkney on board, led until they both came a cropper at the 20th fence. Seven of the 39 horses completed the four and a half miles and Esha Ness ridden by John White and trained by Jenny Pitman crossed the line first. White said, "I could see there were only a few horses around, but I thought the others had fallen or something." Adrian Maguire who rode Romany King said, "Going to The Chair, I wondered what the hell was going on because I saw a fellow wandering nonchalantly across the fence. There were two cones in front of it, but the horses still in the race all kept going." Had the result stood, it would have been the second-fastest time in National history. Peter O'Sullevan commentated, "So as they race up to the line, in the National that surely isn't, Esha Ness is the winner, second is Cahervillahow, third is Romany King, four The Committee and five is Givus A Buck. Then comes On The Other Hand and Laura's Beau and they are the only ones to have completed in the race that surely never was."

A stewards' inquiry declared the race void – for the only time in Grand National history. The Jockey Club decided not to re-run the race and bookies had to refund £75million of wagers. Peter O'Sullevan called it "the greatest disaster in the history of the Grand National". A Jockey Club inquiry led by High Court judge Sir Michael Connell placed some blame on starter Keith Brown but put most of it on Ken Evans, the recall official.

ONLY

WOMAN JOCKEY TO WIN A US TRIPLE CROWN RACE

Julie Krone, Colonial Affair, Belmont Stakes, Belmont Park Racecourse,
2150 Hempstead Turnpike, Elmont, New York 11003, United States.
Saturday 5 June 1993.

Julieann Louise Krone was born on 24 July 1963 at Benton Harbor,
Michigan. After starting as a show jumper, she became a professional
Thoroughbred jockey. Her first ride was on 30 January 1981 at Tampa
Bay Downs, Florida, aboard Tiny Star and her first victory came 13 days
later on Lord Farkle at the same racecourse. In 1993, she won the Belmont
Stakes on 13/1 Colonial Affair, the only woman to win a US Triple Crown
race. Colonial Affair was foaled on 19 April 1990 by Pleasant Colony, out
of Snuggle. He died at Haras El Paraiso in Capitan Sarmiento, Argentina
on 23 April 2013. In 2000, she became **the first woman inducted into the
National Museum of Racing and Hall of Fame**.

ONLY

OPPORTUNITY KNOCKS WINNER TO OWN A GRAND NATIONAL-WINNING HORSE

*Freddie Starr, Opportunity Knocks, Thames TV, Teddington Lock, Broom
Road, London TW11 9NW. 1967; Grand National, Aintree Racecourse,
Ormskirk Road, Aintree, Liverpool L9 5AS. Saturday 9 April 1994.*

Liverpudlian Freddie Starr began his show business career aged 15 with a
small role in *Violent Playground* (1958), a film directed by Basil Dearden.
He joined the Merseybeat group The Midnighters in the early 1960s.
In May 1963, Freddie Starr And The Midnighters released the single
'Who Told You', produced by Joe Meek. Four years later, he appeared
on *Opportunity Knocks*, the talent show hosted by Hughie Green, as part

of the comedy/beat act Freddie Starr and The Delmonts and won the popular vote six weeks in a row. Starr had a topsy-turvy career over the next 40 years with numerous ups and downs including allegations of animal cruelty and sexual impropriety, bankruptcy, TV stardom, drug addiction, reality television and ill health. In 1994, his horse Miinnehoma, ridden by Richard Dunwoody and trained by Martin Pipe, won the 147th Grand National by one and a quarter lengths. Miinnehoma was foaled in 1983, the son of Kambalda (b. 1970) and Mrs Cairns (b. 1974). The following year, again ridden by Dunwoody, Miinnehoma pulled up before the 21st fence on the second circuit of the Grand National. Retired from racing, Miinnehoma lived out his days at Martin Pipe's stables in Wellington, Somerset before his death, aged 29, in July 2012. Freddie Starr died in Spain on 9 May 2019, following a heart attack.

LAST
DERBY FOR LESTER PIGGOTT

EPSOM RACECOURSE, TATTENHAM CORNER ROAD, EPSOM, SURREY KT18 5LQ. WEDNESDAY 1 JUNE 1994.

The 36th and last running for the housewives' favourite Lester Piggott came on the 33/1 Khamaseen. There was to be no successful end to his Derby career as he finished fifth on the John Dunlop-trained horse although another mount trained by John Dunlop, the 7/2 favourite Erhaab ridden by Willie Carson, won by one and a quarter lengths.

LAST
WIN FOR VINCENT O'BRIEN

MYSTERIOUS WAYS, THE CURRAGH, NEWBRIDGE, COUNTY KILDARE R56 RR67 REPUBLIC OF IRELAND. SATURDAY 17 SEPTEMBER 1994.

After a career lasting 51 years, Vincent O'Brien saddled his last winning horse at The Curragh in September 1994. He retired a month later and spent his last years living between Ireland and Perth, Western Australia where is wife came from. He died, aged 92, on 1 June 2009 at his Irish home in Straffan, County Kildare. Racing commentator Brough Scott said, "If the word genius can ever be used when speaking of the conditioning of a Thoroughbred, then it is completely appropriate for Vincent O'Brien. He internationalised the game and completely changed the perception of what horse racing could be, in Ireland, England, and the world."

FIRST
DERBY RUN ON A SATURDAY

EPSOM RACECOURSE, TATTENHAM CORNER ROAD, EPSOM, SURREY KT18 5LQ. SATURDAY 10 JUNE 1995.

Until 1995, the Derby was traditionally run on a Wednesday but this year it was moved to a Saturday to give more people the chance to attend or watch on television. With the going good to firm, Walter Swinburn rode 14/1 Lammtarra to victory by a length over 14 other horses in a record two minutes 32.31 seconds – 1.53 seconds inside the previous Derby best. His record would stand for 15 years. Lammtarra was trained by Saeed Bin Suroor and owned by Saeed Maktoum Al Maktoum. Lammtarra was foaled on 2 February 1992, the son of Nijinsky (see 1969) and Snow Bride. He never lost a race and in 1995 won the Derby, King George VI and Queen Elizabeth Stakes and the Prix de l'Arc de Triomphe – one of only two mounts to triumph in all three races. Lammtarra was sick in the run-up to the Derby and nearly did not compete. On the day, he took the lead with two furlongs to go. Lammtarra retired in 1996 and was sold to Japanese breeders for $30 million and put out to stud. On 6 July 2014, Lammtarra died at Dalham Hall, aged 22.

FIRST

TV CHANNEL FOR A SINGLE SPORT

THE RACING CHANNEL. 1995.

The Racing Channel took to the air in 1995 as the world's first TV channel devoted to just one sport. It cost £19.99 per month to watch and attracted as many as 35,000 subscribers. The channel shut down on 31 January 2003.

FIRST

WOMAN JOCKEY TO RIDE IN THE DERBY

Alex Greaves, Epsom Racecourse, Tattenham Corner Road, Epsom, Surrey KT18 5LQ. 2.25pm, Saturday 8 June 1996.

With the going good, 20 horses competed in the 217th Derby and Alex Greaves, aboard the 500/1 outsider Portuguese Lil, became the first female jockey to take part. She came 20th and last but remembered, "The atmosphere is actually different on Derby Day to any other day. Usually, when you're riding you don't really notice the crowd, because you're focused and your mind's on your job, but at Epsom, even when I got to Tattenham Corner, I was still aware of the buzz and the crowds and everything else." Alex Ann Greaves was born in Northallerton on 14 April 1968 into a family of riders. Unsurprisingly, she got into the saddle at an early age but her mother (see 1976) insisted that she do a three-year catering diploma course at Leeds Polytechnic in case her equine career did not work out.

She turned professional at the end of 1989 and rode her first winner, Andrew's First, at Southwell, on 1 December that year. In 1991, she won the Lincoln Handicap on 22/1 chance Amenable, trained by David Barron. In 1997 at the Nunthorpe Stakes, she dead-heated on Ya Malak to **become the first woman to win a Group 1 race in Britain**. On 28

March 2000 at Newcastle, she became **the first woman to fail a drugs test** after the banned diuretic bendrofluazide was found in her system. Facing a Jockey Club disciplinary committee on 3 August 2000, she said that she had taken a permitted prescription drug and she was cleared. She retired in March 2005, having ridden around 300 winners.

It would be another 16 years before the second female jockey rode in the Derby – Hayley Turner on Cavaleiro in 2012 and she also came last. She commented, "One side of the track everyone's wearing top hats and tails and having champagne, and then on the other side of the track you've got a fairground and people having barbecues."

DID YOU KNOW?

In an interview with a tabloid newspaper, Sir Peter O'Sullevan revealed that he probably spent £20,000 annually gambling on horses.

LAST
GRAND NATIONAL COMMENTARY
BY PETER O'SULLEVAN
AINTREE RACECOURSE, ORMSKIRK ROAD, AINTREE, LIVERPOOL L9 5AS. 5PM, MONDAY 7 APRIL 1997.

The 150th running of the National was due to be run at 3.45pm on Saturday 5 April 1997 but was delayed for two days because of an IRA bomb threat at 2.49pm and then another one at 2.52pm. Sixty thousand spectators were evacuated from the course. At 4.14pm, the police carried out two controlled explosions at Aintree. Before the race could be held on the Monday, another bomb threat was made but the police decided that it was a hoax. When it finally got underway, the race was won by 25 lengths by Lord Gyllene ridden by Tony Dobbin in nine minutes, 5.9 seconds. The bomb threats rather overshadowed the final Grand National broadcast by Sir Peter O'Sullevan, who had announced his retirement earlier in the season.

LAST

COMMENTARY BY SIR PETER O'SULLEVAN

HENNESSY COGNAC GOLD CUP, NEWBURY RACECOURSE,
RACECOURSE ROAD, NEWBURY, BERKSHIRE RG14 7NZ. 2.25PM,
SATURDAY 29 NOVEMBER 1997.

Seven months after his last commentary on the Grand National, Sir Peter O'Sullevan commentated on his last race – his 40th and last commentary on the Hennessy Cognac Gold Cup. He was knighted in 1997. Born in Newcastle, County Down, Ireland on 3 March 1918, he worked on the racing desk at the Press Association before his commentating career started with BBC radio in 1946. The winner of the Hennessy Gold Cup in 1997 from a field of 13 other horses was number 3 Suny Bay, the 9/4 favourite, ridden by Graham Bradley and trained by Charlie Brooks, the husband of News UK chief executive Rebekah Brooks. It was O'Sullevan's last commentary on BBC's *Grandstand*. He died of lung cancer at his flat, 37 Cranmer Court, Whiteheads Grove, Chelsea, London SW3 3HW, on 29 July 2015. He was 97.

ONLY

HORSE TO WIN SCOTTISH GRAND NATIONAL, WELSH GRAND NATIONAL AND GRAND NATIONAL

Earth Summit, Scottish Grand National, Ayr Racecourse, Whitletts Road, Ayr KA8 0JE Scotland. 4.05pm, Saturday 16 April 1994; Welsh Grand National, Chepstow Racecourse, St Lawrence Road, Piercefield Park, Chepstow NP16 6BE Wales. 1.55pm, Saturday 27 December 1997; Grand National, Aintree Racecourse, Ormskirk Road, Aintree, Liverpool L9 5AS. 3.45pm, Saturday 4 April 1998.

Earth Summit was foaled in 1988, the son of Celtic Cone and Win Green Hill. He began racing when he was four. Two years later, he won the

Scottish Grand National ridden by David Bridgwater over four miles one furlong. There were 22 horses in the race, 13 finished and Earth Summit won in eight minutes 20.80 seconds. In February 1996, Earth Summit was badly injured at Haydock and the prognostication for his recovery was not good. However, he survived and thrived. In December 1997, with Tom Jenks on his back, at odds of 25/1 he won the Grand National, clearing 22 fences in heavy going. There were 14 runners and riders and seven completed the three miles and six-and-a-half-furlongs course. Four months later, he made history by winning the Grand National. The 7/1 favourite Earth Summit, ridden by Carl Llewellyn in place of the injured Tom Jenks, was neck and neck with Suny Bay for much of the last third of the race when he took the lead before the second last and went on to win by 11 lengths in ten minutes and 51½ seconds. The 1998 Grand National was the 151st running. There were 37 starters but only six finished the Aintree course and three were injured fatally during the race. The race had the smallest attendance – 46,679 – since 1985, not helped by the bomb threat of the previous year that caused the race to be postponed (see 1997). The going was soft after heavy rain in the morning. Earth Summit retired in 2000 and fell ill in March 2005. A vet discovered cancer in his liver and spleen and he was put down on 23 March 2005.

——•◦•◦•——

FIRST

GRAND NATIONAL SHOWN IN CHINA

AINTREE RACECOURSE, ORMSKIRK ROAD, AINTREE,
LIVERPOOL L9 5AS. 3.45PM, SATURDAY 7 APRIL 2001.

The 2001 Grand National was the 154th and took place amid a foot-and-mouth disease outbreak that had caused the cancellation of the Cheltenham Festival and several other racing meets. There were 40 runners and riders at the start and just four finished in the heavy going. Eight horses fell at the first Canal Turn (the eighth fence). Edmond, the winner of the 1999 Welsh National and 10/1 joint favourite, led for most of the first circuit until he fell into the ditch at The Chair. After the 18th fence, two riderless horses got in the way of Blowing Wind, Brave Highlander and Papillon, forcing all three to refuse. With just three horses still in the competition, it became two when Carl Llewellyn's reins broke on Beau and he fell off. Jockeys A.P. "Tony" McCoy and Ruby Walsh got back on their horses Blowing Wind and Papillon. McCoy later commented, "I looked up at the big screen and saw there were only two horses still racing. I shouted to Ruby, 'Come on, let's get back up.'" They finished third and fourth respectively. Red Marauder managed to overtake Smarty ridden by Timmy Murphy to win by a distance.

It was the first time since 1980 when Ben Nevis won that just four horses completed the race and the first time since 1967 that only two horses finished without being hampered. It was the first time the race was broadcast in communist China and William Hill had managed to get approval for its online bookmaker to be active. The company was expecting good things but had underestimated the traditions and superstitions of the Chinese. Rather than studying form, the Chinese punters picked a horse in their favourite colour. So William Hill had to pay out to 2,000 Chinese gamblers who had bet on 33/1 Red Marauder whose jockey wore silks that were predominantly red.

DID YOU KNOW?

Jockey Paul Flynn was chosen to ride Esprit De Cotte after the original rider Mick Fitzgerald was forced to give up his saddle fewer than two hours before the race. Flynn's mobile was called and several texts sent but to no effect. Tannoy announcements were made but still the errant jockey who had never ridden in the Grand National before did not respond. The BBC which was covering the race put out special calls over the air but still no Flynn and, in the end, Tom Doyle took his place on Esprit De Cotte. The horse refused at the 11th and threw Doyle. Flynn was never given another opportunity to take part in the Grand National.

LAST

COMMENTARY BY PETER BROMLEY

DERBY, EPSOM RACECOURSE, TATTENHAM CORNER
ROAD, EPSOM, SURREY KT18 5LQ. SATURDAY 9 JUNE 2001

For 40 years Peter Bromley was the voice of BBC racing. He announced his decision to stand down when he hit 70 in 1999 but stayed on for another two years. The last race was the 222nd Derby in which the 11/4 joint favourite Galileo, ridden by Michael Kinane, beat Golan with Pat Eddery on board. In retirement, Bromley moved to Suffolk but soon developed pancreatic cancer and died of the disease on 3 June 2003. He was 74.

ONLY

RACING COMMENTATOR TO APPEAR ON CELEBRITY BIG BROTHER

John McCririck, Celebrity Big Brother, *Channel 4, Elstree Studios, Shenley Road, Borehamwood, Hertfordshire WD6 1JG. Thursday 6 January to Monday 17 January 2005.*

Celebrity Big Brother began on Channel 4 on 9 March 2001 as a spin-off version of reality programme *Big Brother.* It was supposed to be a one-off but was successful enough to warrant an occasional series. Racing commentator John McCririck appeared on the third series, which began on 6 January 2005. He was the first housemate to go into the house. He did not endear himself to his fellow housemates, accusing the American model Caprice of just appearing in the show to make money and to promote her lingerie line. He had an argument with Big Brother over not receiving his promised Diet Coke. On Day 12, he became the second housemate to be evicted. In 2010, he went back into the house as a contestant on *Ultimate Big Brother*, where he was the first housemate to be evicted. He died on 5 July 2019, aged 79.

ONLY

GRAND NATIONAL DELAYED BY A ROYAL WEDDING

AINTREE RACECOURSE, ORMSKIRK ROAD, AINTREE, LIVERPOOL L9 5AS. 4.10PM, SATURDAY 9 APRIL 2005.

The wedding of HRH The Prince of Wales and Mrs Andrew Parker Bowles had already been delayed by one day because of the funeral of HH Pope John Paul II. Due to take place on Friday 8 April, the ceremony had to be pushed back a day so Prince Charles could attend the Holy Father's interment. The Royal Wedding went ahead at the Windsor Guildhall at 12.30pm. The Grand National start time was pushed back by 25 minutes. The race was won by 14 lengths in nine minutes 21 seconds by the nine-year-old 7/1 favourite Hedgehunter, ridden by Ruby Walsh and trained by Willie Mullins. Hedgehunter, the first horse in 17 years to carry 11 stone or more and win, was foaled in the early hours of 28 January 1996 on the Tully Hill Stud in Dublin. He ran in five Grand Nationals and retired on 10 April 2008. He died on 25 January 2023.

ONLY

PAGE 3 PHOTOGRAPHER TO BREED A DERBY WINNER

Harry Ormesher, Sir Percy, Epsom Racecourse, Tattenham Corner Road, Epsom, Surrey KT18 5LQ. Saturday 3 June 2006.

Born on 10 May 1934, Harry Ormesher worked as a glamour photographer and nightclub owner before giving it all up when he was 62 to try to breed a Derby winner. It was a childhood passion and he grew up watching his father own, breed and race horses. When he was 12, he revealed, "The first decent picture I took was of a horse and it won a prize in a local show competition."

In May 1960, he opened The Iron Door Club at 13 Temple Street, Liverpool with Geoff Hogarth. It had a capacity of 1,650 people. On 15 May 1960, it was the first venue The Beatles played using that name (actually The Silver Beetles). The night before, they played Lathom Hall in Liverpool as the Silver Beats. The club closed in 1964. He was the official snapper for Liverpool, photographing their first European Cup triumph in 1977 and the Heysel Stadium disaster in May 1985. He worked in Fleet Street taking pictures of celebrities and topless women.

Ormesher bought his first Flat racehorse in 1993 and in 1997 he put in everything he had to open Old Suffolk Stud in Hundon, Suffolk. Sir Percy was foaled on 27 January 2003, the son of Mark of Esteem (winner of the 1996 2000 Guineas) and Percy's Lass (died 1988). His damsire, Blakeney (named after Sir Percy Blakeney, the hero of Baroness Orczy's 1905 novel *The Scarlet Pimpernel*) won the Derby in 1969. At birth, Sir Percy immediately kicked the breeder in the head. Ormesher recalled, "His legs were flying everywhere but all he wanted to do was get out. He has been like that all his life, wanting to get on and do everything as quickly as possible. I have still never seen a foal gallop like he did."

Sir Percy began his racing career on 28 May 2005 with a win at Goodwood and won five out of his ten starts. In 2006, Sir Percy won the Derby as 6/1 third favourite coming out best of a four-way photo finish. Ormesher picked up the Breeders' Trophy and £10,000 in prize money. In June 2007, Sir Percy was put out to stud at Kirsten Rausing's Lanwades Stud in Newmarket after failing to win three races. Ormesher died on 12 November 2015.

ONLY

BRITISH MONARCH TO ATTEND KENTUCKY DERBY

HM QUEEN ELIZABETH II, CHURCHILL DOWNS RACECOURSE, 700
CENTRAL AVENUE, LOUISVILLE, KENTUCKY 40208 UNITED STATES OF
AMERICA. SATURDAY 5 MAY 2007.

In her first visit to the former colony since 1991, The Queen attended the
Kentucky Derby and watched Street Sense ridden by Calvin Borel win the
133rd running, the first of his three Derby wins.

FIRST

WOMAN TO RIDE 100 UK FLAT RACE WINNERS IN A CALENDAR YEAR

**Hayley Turner, Wolverhampton Racecourse, Dunstall Park,
Gorsebrook Road, Wolverhampton, West Midlands WV6 0PE.
Tuesday 30 December 2008.**

Hayley Turner is regarded as the first woman to have a professional
career as a jockey in the UK. She was born on 3 January 1983 and
hails from Nottingham. She began riding at an early age and her first
race was on Markellis at Southwell on 27 March 2000. Turner never
finished the race as her mount broke a leg and had to be put down. On
4 June 2000, she rode her first winner but did not win another race until
2002. Then she suddenly began building up the number of wins before
achieving her century at Wolverhampton on 30 December 2008 riding
Mullitovermaurice. In 2012, she was just eight short of repeating her best
season. On 2 June 2012, she was the second female jockey to ride in the
Derby, coming last on Cavaleiro. Her appearance in the Derby caused
chatter in the wider world but, inside the sport, she said it was a regular
thing, adding, "Trainers and jockeys thought it was quite normal, because
we do it every day – they had accepted us as jockeys – but for everyone else
looking in, it was a big deal."

LAST

THRILLER BY DICK FRANCIS

Even Money, *Michael Joseph, London. Tuesday 25 August 2009.*

Jockey turned thriller writer Dick Francis died on St Valentine's Day 2010 in Grand Cayman. The last book was *Even Money*, which appeared in 2009. His son Felix Francis has carried on writing "Dick Francis" novels. Dick Francis's novels, whoever wrote them, have been published in 35 languages, sold more than 60 million copies and won a number of prizes.

FIRST

JOCKEY TO WIN
BBC SPORTS PERSONALITY OF THE YEAR AWARD

TONY McCOY, BBC ONE, LG ARENA, PERIMETER ROAD,
BIRMINGHAM B40 1NT. SUNDAY 19 DECEMBER 2010.

Instigated in 1954 by Paul Fox, it took 56 years for a jockey to win the trophy – Frankie Dettori came third in 1996, McCoy finished third in 2002 (on 2 April that year, he beat Sir Gordon Richards's all-time record of 269 winners in a season – he finished on 289) and would finish in the same place in 2013. In 2010, he won 41.98 per cent of the vote – 293,152 in total. He said, "This is an unbelievable feeling standing here in front of all these amazing people. It's not something that anyone would be silly enough to dream about, even me. My daughter, Eve, who is three, was shouting at me when she knew I was going to be on television this evening. I want to keep going now. I want to be a Champion Jockey and I want to be at the top of my sport. I don't know how long I will go on – time is the enemy of any sportsman."

Sir A.P. McCoy was born on 4 May 1974 at Moneyglass, County Antrim, Northern Ireland and won his first race, Legal Steps at Thurles, on 26 March 1992 when he was aged 17. He turned professional in 1995 and retired in 2015 – being Champion Jockey every year that he was a professional. On 9 February 2009, he rode his 3,000th winner Restless D'Artaix in the Tyser & Co Beginners' Chase in the 4.20pm at Plumpton. In 2010, he won the Grand National at the 15th attempt, riding Don't Push It. He rode a record 4,358 winners – his 4,000th winner coming at Towcester on 7 November 2013 when he guided Mountain Tunes to victory. He was knighted in January 2016.

ONLY

JOCKEY TO APPEAR ON
I'm A Celebrity Get Me Out Of Here

Willie Carson, I'm A Celebrity Get Me Out Of Here,
ITV, Murwillumbah, New South Wales, Australia.
Sunday 13 November to Saturday 3 December 2011.

Having been the first jockey team captain on *A Question Of Sport* (see 1982), in 2011 Willie Carson became the only jockey to appear on celebrity reality show *I'm A Celebrity Get Me Out Of Here*. On 1 December 2011, he finished fifth, being the eighth person to be kicked out of camp. His campmates were the winner Dougie Poynter, runner-up Mark Wright, bronze medallist Fatima Whitbread, fourth Antony Cotton, sixth Crissy Rock, seventh Emily Scott, eighth Jessica-Jane Clement, ninth Lorraine Chase, tenth Pat Sharp, 11th Sinitta, and 12th and last Stefanie Powers. Freddie Starr (see 1994) pulled out on 15 November 2011 after becoming too ill to continue.

FIRST

GRAND NATIONAL WITH A SEVEN-FIGURE PRIZE FUND

Aintree Racecourse, Ormskirk Road, Aintree, Liverpool L9 5AS.
4.18pm, Saturday 5 April 2014.

The 167th Grand National was the first in which the 40 horses competed for a share of the £1 million prize fund. The race was won by the 25/1 outsider Pineau De Re ridden by Leighton Aspell, who came out of retirement for the race, and trained by Dr Richard Newland. Triumphing by five lengths, Pineau De Re was the sixth French-bred horse to win the Grand National. Eighteen of the 40 mounts finished the race and there were no fatalities. Despite encouragement, the 40/1 Battle Group refused to join the starting line-up and was ruled out. Commentator Simon Holt described the race's finish, "Pineau De Re and Leighton Aspell, chased hard by Balthazar King and Richard Johnson and by Double Seven and A.P. McCoy. But at the elbow, it's Pineau De Re by six lengths. Inside the final furlong, Balthazar King, and after him Double Seven as they race up towards the line. Pineau De Re, the 11-year-old for trainer Dr Richard Newland and Leighton Aspell is going to take out the Crabbie's Grand National! Pineau De Re wins, Balthazar King second, Double Seven third."

ONLY
BREEDERS' CUP GRAND SLAM WINNER

American Pharoah, Kentucky Derby, Churchill Downs Racecourse, 700 Central Avenue, Louisville, Kentucky 40208 United States of America. 6.44pm, Saturday 2 May 2015; American Pharoah, Preakness Stakes, Pimlico Racecourse, 5201 Park Heights Avenue, Baltimore, Maryland 21215 United States of America. Saturday 16 May 2015; American Pharoah, Belmont Stakes, Belmont Park Racecourse, 2150 Hempstead Turnpike, Elmont, New York 11003 United States of America. 6.52pm Saturday 6 June 2015; Breeders' Cup, Keeneland Racecourse, 4201 Versailles Road, Lexington, Kentucky 40510-9648 United States of America. Saturday 31 October 2015.

There are two ways to win the Grand Slam or Quadruple Crown in American racing. One is to win the Triple Crown and then the Travers while the other is the Triple Crown and then the Breeders' Cup. Each way has only been achieved once. American Pharoah won the Breeders' Cup Grand Slam in 2015, 74 years after Whirlaway (see 1941) won the Travers. American Pharoah was trained by Bob Baffert and ridden by Victor Espinoza.

A record 170,513 crowd went to Churchill Downs for the 141st Kentucky Derby on a warm day. American Pharoah was the 5/2 favourite. There were 18 runners and riders. Dortmund and Firing Line were the early leaders with American Pharoah just behind and he took the lead in the home stretch. He held on to win by a length in two minutes 3.02 seconds. It was the third Derby win for Espinoza (and the second in a row, having won in 2014 on California Chrome) and the fourth for horse Baffert. The jockey and the trainer had won the 2002 Kentucky Derby with War Emblem.

A fortnight later, it was the Preakness Stakes. Just eight horses lined up for the 140th running – the smallest in 15 years – before a crowd of 131,680. The going was heavy thanks to a thunderstorm before the race. It was the first time the race had taken place in those conditions since 1983. The grandstands were evacuated just before the off as authorities worried about lightning strikes. American Pharoah took the lead early on and, apart from an early challenge by Mr Z and later by Dortmund and Divining Rod, never lost it and won by seven lengths. American Pharoah's winning time of one minute 58.46 seconds was the slowest since Hill Prince won in 1950.

The 147th Belmont Stakes was the third leg of the Triple Crown and Grand Slam and came three weeks after the Preakness. Expecting a huge crowd to see a potential Triple Crown, the New York Racing Association limited the crowd to 90,000. Eight horses lined up and in previous contests American Pharoah had beaten them all. That day would be no exception as American Pharoah covered the one-and-a-half-mile course in two minutes 26.65 seconds – the sixth-fastest of all time – winning by five and a half lengths. American Pharoah became the 12th winner of the US Triple Crown. NBC commentator Larry Collmus said, "And they're into the stretch, and American Pharoah makes his run for glory as they come into the final furlong! Frosted is second with one eighth of a mile to go! American Pharoah's got a two-length lead! Frosted is all out at the 16th pole! And here it is! The 37-year wait is over! American Pharoah is finally the one! American Pharoah has won the Triple Crown!" Victor Espinoza became the first Latino jockey to win the Triple Crown and, at age 43, he was also the oldest.

On Hallowe'en 2015, American Pharoah went to Lexington, Kentucky to race in the Breeders' Cup – his last race before retirement – to see if he could win the Grand Slam. There was $5 million at stake as well as a place in the history books. American Pharoah was the 3/5 favourite among the crowd of 50,155 at Keeneland – the first time the race had been held there. The Triple Crown champion, ridden by Victor Espinoza, ran the one and a quarter miles in a track record of two minutes 0.07 seconds, winning by six and a half lengths. Espinoza said, "I was trying to open it up as much as I can. I saw the wire maybe 20 yards [away], and for me it was not coming fast enough because I want to cross that wire and get it over with." In the winner's enclosure, the crowds surrounded the three-year-old colt clapping and cheering but he did not hear them. He wore ear plugs to muffle any noises that might startle him. Trainer Bob Baffert said, "It's a lot of pressure to train a horse like this because I didn't want to let the horse down and I didn't want to let the fans down. I'm just so proud of him; it's like watching my child out there." American Pharoah won nine of his 11 career starts, including the first sweep of the Kentucky Derby, Preakness and Belmont in 37 years.

━━◆━◆◆◆━◆━━

FIRST
WOMAN JOCKEY TO RIDE IN THE DERBY
AND NOT COME LAST

ANASTASIA O'BRIEN, EPSOM RACECOURSE, TATTENHAM CORNER ROAD, EPSOM, SURREY KT18 5LQ. SATURDAY 3 JUNE 2017.

With the going good, 18 horses competed in the 238th Derby and Ana O'Brien, aboard the 66/1 The Anvil, became the first woman jockey to compete in the Derby and manage to finish ahead of a male jockey. O'Brien finished 17th ahead of 100/1 Pealer, ridden by Sylvester De Sousa. The race was shown on ITV for the first time since 1988. No woman has won the Derby.

FIRST
FEMALE JOCKEY TO WIN
THE GRAND NATIONAL
ONLY
GRAND NATIONAL WITH NO SPECTATORS

RACHAEL BLACKMORE, AINTREE RACECOURSE, ORMSKIRK ROAD, AINTREE, LIVERPOOL L9 5AS. SATURDAY 10 APRIL 2021.

Due to the Covid-19 epidemic, the 2020 Grand National was cancelled and, for 2021, there were no spectators at Aintree to watch the 173rd race. There were 40 runners and riders and the favourite was Cloth Cap at 11/2, ridden by Tom Scudamore and trained by Jonjo O'Neill. By 2021, 19 women had ridden in the National with varying degrees of success. Of the 14 attempts between 1977 and 1989, only Geraldine Rees had managed to stay the course. There were no female competitors from 1990 to 1993 and then Rosemary Henderson finished fifth on Fiddlers Pike in 1994.

Another hiatus occurred until Carrie Ford came fifth on Forest Gunner in 2005. The following year, Nina Carberry took the reins and came ninth on Forest Gunner. Another hiatus followed until 2010 when Carberry finished seventh on Character Building and then raced again on the same horse in 2011 but finished 15th on this occasion. On 14 April 2012, Carberry made her fourth attempt but she fell off Organisedconfusion at the eighth fence (Canal Turn).

Katie Walsh achieved the best women's result that year, coming third on Seabass. It was a false dawn because, although female jockeys raced in 2013, 2014, 2015, 2016, 2017, 2018 and 2019, no one achieved a better finish than fifth – Bryony Frost in 2018 on Milansbar. That was the same year that Rachael Blackmore first raced in the National on Alpha Des Obeaux but the 33/1 horse fell over at The Chair. Blackmore was back in 2019 on Valseur Lido and finished tenth. In 2021, she made her third appearance – this time on 11/1 Minella Times, trained by Henry de Bromhead. In March 2021, Blackmore became **the first woman leading jockey at the Cheltenham Festival**.

Blackmore was born at Killenaule, County Tipperary, Ireland on 11 July 1989 and raised on a dairy farm. On 10 February 2011, Blackmore won her first race as an amateur jockey when Stowaway Pearl won the Tipperary Ladies' Handicap Hurdle at Thurles. She turned professional in March 2015. At the National where the going was good to soft, Blackmore was one of three female jockeys in the race. There were 37 men racing. Cloth Cap took the lead but was caught by Jett who took a big lead, with Cloth Cap remaining in second for much of the race. Cloth Cap was pulled up four fences from the finish. The Long Mile injured himself on the flat running between fences and had to be put down. Approaching the third-last fence, Jett faded and was caught by Minella Times, Any Second Now, Discorama, Burrows Saint and Balko Des Flos. At the penultimate fence Minella Times grabbed the lead and held on to win by six and a half lengths. Blackmore said, "I cannot believe it. He was a sensational spin. It is unbelievable. I don't feel male or female. I don't even feel human, I feel unbelievable."

LAST
AMATEUR JOCKEY TO WIN GRAND NATIONAL

SAM WALEY-COHEN, NOBLE YEATS, AINTREE RACECOURSE, ORMSKIRK ROAD, AINTREE, LIVERPOOL L9 5AS. SATURDAY 9 APRIL 2022.

The last amateur jockey to win was Sam Waley-Cohen with 50/1 Noble Yeats in 2022 beating 15/2 favourite Any Second Now by two and a quarter lengths. Waley-Cohen was the first amateur to win since Marcus Armytage won on Mr Frisk in 1990. He is also **the first amateur jockey to ride the winner of the Grand National and the Cheltenham Gold Cup**. He won the Cheltenham Gold Cup on Long Run in 2011. His father's horse, Noble Yeats, was the first seven-year-old to win the race since Bogskar in 1940. Waley-Cohen's tenth and last Grand National, in 2022, was not without a bittersweet memory. He was suspended for nine days and fined £400 for using his whip above the permitted level after the last fence and in the incorrect place on the run to the line.

DID YOU KNOW?

Away from the turf, Sam Waley-Cohen is a successful businessman. He hails from a privileged background. The founder of Shell Oil, Marcus Samuel, 1st Viscount Bearsted, was his great-great-grandfather. His grandfather Sir Bernard Waley-Cohen was the Lord Mayor of London in 1960. His aunt Joanna Waley-Cohen is the Provost for New York University Shanghai and Silver Professor of History at New York University. His father, Robert, founded diagnostic imaging business Alliance Medical in 1989. Sam Waley-Cohen was at boarding school with HRH the Princess of Wales and was credited with getting her and Prince William back together after they split in March 2007. He founded the Portman Dentalcare chain of dental practices in 2009. By 2023, he ran more than 350 practices, with 2,000 clinicians and 4,000 employees.

The 2022 National was also **the first time that more than half the horses had been trained in Ireland**. He retired after the race. Rather than the usual 30 fences, only 29 fences were jumped because there was a medical emergency at the 19th fence. Discorama and Eclair Surf were put down after suffering injuries in the race. In 2007, he came fifth on Liberthine, his father's horse. Two years later, he fell at the second fence on Ollie Magern. In 2011, he rode Oscar Time for the first time in the National and finished second. In 2013, he and Oscar Time finished fourth. The next year, he and Long Run fell at the ninth. Back on Oscar Time in 2015, he finished 15th. In 2016, on Black Thunder he was pulled up at the 21st fence. He fell at the sixth on The Young Master in 2017 and then took a four-year hiatus until 2021 when he came eighth on Jett.

FIRST

FEMALE TRAINER TO WIN A US TRIPLE CROWN RACE

JENA M. ANTONUCCI, ARCANGELO, BELMONT STAKES, BELMONT PARK RACECOURSE, 2150 HEMPSTEAD TURNPIKE, ELMONT, NEW YORK 11003 UNITED STATES OF AMERICA. 6.50PM, SATURDAY 10 JUNE 2023.

The 155th Belmont Stakes took place on the second Saturday in June 2023. It was the third and final leg of the American Triple Crown although no horse could win the Crown because different horses had won the Kentucky Derby and Preakness. Nine horses began the Belmont Stakes and Arcangelo came home in two minutes 29.23 seconds. Ridden by Javier Castellano, Arcangelo was trained by Jena M. Antonucci – the first woman trainer to win a US Triple Crown race. Arcangelo held off a late run by Forte and gave Castellano his first Belmont win in 14 attempts. Antonucci was asked what the victory meant to her and said, "I don't have a polished answer. They say no crying in baseball, I think it's the same in horse racing. Horses don't know who you are. To have a horse believe in you and your team like this one does, I wish more people can be like horses."

Bibliography

Books

Bailey, Philip, Philip Thorn and Peter Wynne-Thomas *Who's Who Of Cricketers* (London: Newnes Books, 1983)

Barrett, Norman *The Daily Telegraph Chronicle Of Horse Racing* (Enfield: Guinness Publishing, 1995)

Beadle, Jeremy *Jeremy Beadle's Today's The Day* (London: W.H. Allen, 1979)

Betz, Paul and Mark C. Carnes (Eds) *American National Biography Supplement 1* (New York: Oxford University Press, 2002)

Brahms, William B. *Notable Last Facts* (New Jersey: Reference Desk Press, 2005)

Cottrell, John and Marcus Armytage *A-Z Of The Grand National* (Newbury, Berkshire: Highdown, 2009)

Crewe, The Marquess of *Lord Rosebery* (London: John Murray, 1931)

Donnelley, Paul *Firsts, Lasts & Onlys: Football* (London: Hamlyn, 2010)

—— *The Notorious Guide To Britain* (London: Mardle Books, 2022)

Foulkes, Nicholas *Gentlemen And Blackguards* (London: Phoenix, 2011)

Francis, Dick *The Sport Of Queens* (London: Pan Books, 1983)

Gilbert, Martin *Prophet Of Truth Winston S. Churchill 1922-1939* (London: Minerva, 1990)

Gilbey, Quentin *Queen Of The Turf The Dorothy Paget Story* (London: Arthur Barker, 1973)

Green, Reg *The History Of The Grand National* (London: Hodder & Stoughton, 1993)

Herbert, Ivor *Red Rum: The Full And Extraordinary Story Of A Horse Of Courage* (London: William Luscombe, 1974)

Higham, Charles *Dark Lady Winston Churchill's Mother And Her World* (London: Virgin, 2006)

Holland, Anne *Classic Horse Races Famous Moments From The History Of The Flat, Steeplechase And Hurdles* (London: Queen Anne Press, 1991)

Jackson, Kenneth T. (Ed) *The Encyclopedia Of New York City* (New Haven: Yale University Press, 1995)

James, Robert Rhodes *Rosebery: A Biography Of Archibald Philip, Fifth Earl Of Rosebery* (London: Weidenfeld & Nicolson, 1963)

Karter, John *Lester Return Of A Legend* (London: Headline, 1993)

Kemper, Steve *A Splendid Savage The Restless Life Of Frederick Russell Burnham* (New York: W.W. Norton, 2016)

Lacey, Robert *Great Tales From English History The Battle Of The Boyne To DNA 1690-1953* (London: Little, Brown, 2006)

Matthew, H.G.C. and Brian Harrison *Oxford Dictionary Of National Biography* (Oxford: Oxford University Press, 2004)

McKinstry, Leo *Rosebery Statesman In Turmoil* (London: John Murray, 2005)

Mooney, Bill and George Ennor *The Complete Encyclopaedia Of Horse Racing* (London: Carlton Books, 2007)

Mortimer, Roger, Richard Onslow and Peter Willett *Biographical Encyclopaedia Of British Flat Racing* (McDonald & Jane's, 1978)

Mosley, Charles *Burke's Peerage Baronetage & Knightage* (107th Edition) (Wilmington, Delaware: Burke's Peerage & Gentry LLC, 2003)

Murray, Amanda *Race To The Finish The Life And Times Of Fred Archer* (London: Robson Books, 2003)

Piggott, Lester *Lester The Autobiography Of Lester Piggott* (London: Partridge Press, 1995)

Pope-Hennessy, James *Queen Mary* (London: George Allen and Unwin, 1959)

Read, Phyllis J. and Bernard L. Witlieb *The Book Of Women's Firsts* (New York: Random House, 1992)

Robertson, Patrick *The Guinness Book Of Australian Firsts* (Sydney, Australia: Collins, Australia and Guinness Superlatives, 1987)

——-*The New Shell Book Of Firsts* (London: Headline, 1994)

——-*Robertson's Book Of Firsts* (New York: Bloomsbury USA, 2011)

Sebba, Anne Jennie *Churchill Winston's American Mother* (London: John Murray, 2007)

Sharpe, Graham *Turf Accounts* (Enfield: Guinness Publishing, 1990)

Smith, Vian *The Grand National* (London: Stanley Paul, 1962)

Stratman, Linda *The Marquess Of Queensberry Wilde's Nemesis* (New Haven, Connecticut: Yale University Press, 2013)

Taaffe, Pat *My Life & Arkle's* (London: Stanley Paul, 1972)

White, John *The Horse Racing Miscellany* (Third Edition) (London: Sevenoaks, 2016)

Winn, Christopher *I Never Knew That About The Irish* (London: Ebury Press, 2009)

Wright, Howard *The Encyclopaedia Of Flat Racing* (Second Edition) (London: Robert Hale, 1986)

Zilboorg, Caroline (Ed) *Women's Firsts* (Detroit: Gale Research, 1997)

Newspapers

Daily Express; Daily Mirror; Daily Record; Irish Examiner; Daily Telegraph; The Independent; The Los Angeles Times; The New York Times; The Northern Echo; The Sun; The Sydney Morning Herald; York Press

Websites

Baird Television

BBC

Betting-Offers

Courier-Journal

Grand National Guide

Grand National Ultimate History

Greyhound Derby

Jockeypedia
Kentucky Derby
MailOnline
Racing Museum
Racing Post
The Jockey Club
Wikipedia
YouTube